'If anyone is qualified t[...]
to find it. Rachael New[...]
dox that deep joy can o[...] .....…. Rachael makes
joy accessible to people who believe it is beyond their reach.'
The Revd Will van der Hart, founder, Mind and Soul Foundation

'Lament can often be an uncomfortable topic, yet Rachael bravely
and sensitively tackles it head on, showing us the importance of ad-
dressing our pain and wrestling with God. This honest account will
inspire you towards hope, helping you to find joy in the most unexpected places. I highly recommend this book to anyone who needs to
know that there is a "yet" in the midst of their suffering.'
Ruth Jackson, presenter and producer at Premier's *Unbelievable*

'"And yet" – two little words that bind together the twin realities
of grief, depression, sickness and poverty and God's loving, eternal,
comforting presence. Rachael has done fierce battle with her mental
health and chosen to remain engaged with God, discovering along
the way the gift of lament and the joy to which it gives birth. Make
this book your friend – live with it, pray with it, write notes in the
margins and let it lead you into the deep heart-knowledge that you
are not alone.'
Jo Swinney, Director of Communications, A Rocha International,
and author of *Home: The quest to belong*

Rachael Newham is the founder of Christian mental health charity ThinkTwice, and is now Mental Health Friendly Church Project Manager at Kintsugi Hope. She is the author of *Learning to Breathe* (2018) and a contributor to *Hope Rising 365*. She writes and speaks nationally about mental health and faith and can be found on Instagram @RachaelNewham90.

AND YET

Finding joy in lament

Rachael Newham

FORM

First published in Great Britain in 2021

Form
36 Causton Street
London SW1P 4ST
www.spck.org.uk

British Library Cataloguing-in-Publication Data
A catalogue record for this book is available from the British Library

ISBN 978–0–281–08570–5
eBook ISBN 978–0–281–08571–2

Typeset by Manila Typesetting Company
First printed in Great Britain by Ashford Colour Press
Subsequently digitally printed in Great Britain

eBook by Manila Typesetting Company

Produced on paper from sustainable forests

Contents

For

my husband Phil – my partner
on the paths of joy and lament

Foreword

We are often led to portray a perfect image of ourselves. In a world where status and achievements are used as primary measures of self-worth, we learn from a young age that some things are just better silenced and confined to the privacy of our own heart. And yet, integrity for me is one of the most attractive values. What I love about the book in your hands is that it's honest and real and shows how God meets us in the everyday moments of life and especially in the hard times; the author embodies this integrity too.

I have had the pleasure of getting to know Rachael over the last couple of years and it's not only the way she writes and talks that I find inspirational, but the way she lives. Being honest and vulnerable when your life falls apart is not easy in a society where we are told to pull ourselves together, to focus on the bright side, or not to cry when we feel sad. All this pretending we are OK and suppression of emotions is neither natural nor healthy! Crying when we are sad is healthy and learning to lament is vital. When we don't allow ourselves to go through this natural process of grieving or seasonal brokenness, we deny a fundamental part of our humanity and allow emotions such as anger and bitterness to take root in our heart instead of allowing them to show us what is wrong.

While honesty is a commendable moral value when it comes to telling the truth, or giving back what does not belong to us, it becomes awkward and uncomfortable when it comes to revealing our weaknesses, fears and failures.

This last year most of us have dealt with more fear, more loss, more change and more stress than we could ever have imagined. *And Yet* I have also felt the closeness of God in so many unusual ways that I was not expecting.

I recently had the privilege of speaking to Terry Waite who was held hostage for five years. Terry Waite was working to free hostages when he was taken prisoner in Beirut in 1987. He spent 1,460 days in solitary confinement and then wasn't released for almost another year. The conditions he describes are horrific. Held in a cell, chained to a wall and sleeping on the floor, with no natural light, no companionship and nothing to read, watch or listen to in order to dull the agonizing passage of time. It's impossible to imagine the anguish of such conditions. Especially when he didn't know if or when he might be released or whether he would be held there until his execution.

Many people say that when they're at their lowest, they've known God closest. But that's not true for everyone. Terry says that on one particular day of his captivity he was told he had five hours left to live and was given a mock execution. His captors allowed him to write one letter to his loved ones, and say the Lord's Prayer, then they held a gun to his head. He says:

I felt alone and isolated. I never felt what some people claim to feel and that is the close presence of God. That doesn't mean to say I lost faith because faith is not dependent on feeling. Feeling can be occasioned by illness and all sorts of things but it's not a reliable guide as to whether you have faith. I realized I could say, 'You have the power to break my body (they tried) and my mind (they tried) but my soul is not yours to possess.'

In Terry's words I hear the echo of the Psalms. In my dark times I want to choose to turn towards God in my pain and not turn my back on him.

In this book, Rachael takes us on a journey through the liturgical seasons to explore the interconnectivity of lament and joy. Each chapter is full of biblical insights and real stories. Rachael beautifully interweaves her hopes and fears; through theological reflection and lived experience, she helps us all discover treasure in life's scars.

When you have read this book, pass it on to a friend, or even better buy another copy, as I am sure the stories will inspire and encourage many.

Patrick Regan OBE
Kintsugi Hope

Acknowledgements

They say it takes a village to raise a child – and it turns out it takes a village to write a book too, and it takes the very best of villages to raise a child and a book at the same time!

A massive thank you to Elizabeth Neep and the team at SPCK – the journey to this book was a bit of a whirlwind, but I'm so grateful that Elizabeth believed in me and the book you're now reading so thank you to the wonderful people who made my words into a real-life book.

To the St Andrew's mums who have sustained me through writing this over three lockdowns with video chats, chilly park dates and sanity-saving companionship.

To John and Alice Buckeridge for being some of the most encouraging people on the planet and for giving me more than one helping hand during my career thus far!

To the brilliant team at Kintsugi Hope – I love working alongside such passionate, creative people every day; and special thanks to Patrick for writing the Foreword.

To the ThinkTwice trustees past and present – so much of what I have learned about joy and lament has been through my journey with you all.

Acknowledgements

To all those who have mentored and cheered me on over the past ten years, with special thanks to Al Ronberg and Will van der Hart.

To my most wonderful family: Mum, Dad, Virginia, my in-laws Andrew and Gillian and the whole Newham clan. I so appreciate your encouragement, love and practical help! Without you there would be no book.

And finally, to my Phil and our Sebastian for putting up with long days of me glued to my laptop and for being my greatest joys in life.

Introduction

If writing a book about suicide and depression in my twenties was unexpected, writing a book about joy in my thirties was perhaps even more so – particularly because, as I write, COVID-19 is sweeping through the world. Joy is the furthest thing from most minds. Businesses have closed their doors, shops have shut and schools are open only to a few. The streets of my little village, usually thronging with life and community, are eerily quiet, with anxiety hanging in the air like the smog which has only recently lifted from the skies of emptied cities.

And yet.

There is a sweet scent in the air as the summer blooms break through the darkness of the soil. Life for many is slower. We are appreciating those who work steadfastly in our communities with little thanks, from delivery drivers to supermarket workers. Every Thursday evening a roar of applause breaks through the evening air as people 'Clap for Carers'. An elderly man raises millions of pounds for NHS charities by walking laps of his garden on his Zimmer frame.

Throughout history and Scripture we see the same pattern: the world feels darker than we can manage and yet God is kinder than we could ever have imagined.

Amid our chaotic world, there is a steady drumbeat that marks a rhythm we can follow if only we dare to notice it. The Christian year is made up of seasons which not only allow, but encourage, times to cherish joy and tend to grief individually and communally.

Indeed, each season of celebration in the Christian year is preceded by a time of lament and reflection, reminding us of the need for both in our spiritual lives. The joy and wonder of Christmas is preceded by the longing and waiting of Advent; the victory of the resurrection is preceded by the honesty and lamentation of Lent; and in between there are the spaces of Ordinary Time, which take up most of the year and yet are often overlooked completely. The message I see is that God is in it all: the lament, the joy and the in-between times where we hold joy and sorrow together in an often uncomfortable alliance. God doesn't only show up in our most dramatic times, he is Emmanuel through every valley, every peak and everywhere in-between.

In Paul's letter to the Romans, he exhorts his readers to 'Rejoice with those who rejoice, and weep with those who weep' (Romans 12.15, NKJV) and Paul did not speak from a vacuum, but as one well-acquainted with the joy of salvation and the sorrow of persecution and imprisonment.

These seasons don't mean that we can't or won't experience the opposite feelings during these times; in fact our sorrows and joys can be intensified when we are grieving during times of celebration or celebrating while others grieve. But it does mean that as a community of believers we can come together to process our joy and pain in the presence of God, despite what is going on for us personally.

I, like most people who study lament, began out of necessity. The language of victory and triumph over adversity that I heard in worship songs, the stories told (almost exclusively) at evangelistic events about ailments cured and problems solved, jarred painfully with my own reality. I became a Christian aged five and by the time I was in my early teens and my friends began to go to festivals and give their lives to Jesus, I had developed a depression that would threaten my life. I couldn't reconcile the stories I was hearing from friends about how Christianity made their life better with my own story, which felt as if it started with promise and was getting progressively darker.

I knew I wanted to serve God, but I didn't know how when my tears blinded me. And so, during regular visits to my local Christian bookshop, I began to seek out books which answered the question that was burned into my soul, and perhaps lingers in yours, too. Where is God when it hurts?

I read voraciously, and in the years that followed I probably read more about God than I read from God through the Bible, so while I began to get an intellectual understanding of theodicy (the question of how an all-loving, all-powerful God would allow his creation to suffer), and I continued to love God, there was a gap between my knowledge and my relationship with Jesus. Throughout these years, I wrote extensively in my diary, an A4, pink, hardback book that I'd bought when I was 14 and which would become the record of my descent into mental illness. It was only as I looked back at this that I realized it was full of lament before I even knew what the word was. The prayers were raw and more honest than I was ever able to be with those around me. I lamented to God through my writing, with the vague hope that God was reading my desperate pleas and would act.

By the time I was in my late teens, I'd tried twice to take my own life and was well acquainted with the darkness, but it wasn't until then that I began to learn a language for my pain and outpourings of grief. As I recovered, I received cards with portions of the Psalms carefully copied out, and as I read them I began to recognize my own heartbreak in the ancient words. I began to see that the gap between my knowledge of theology and my relationship with Jesus could be bridged with the honesty of lament.

The Psalms and stories of lament captured my imagination. I began to learn what it looked like to lament outside the bounds of my own heart and mind. While studying first for my undergraduate dissertation looking at a pastoral theology of suicidal thoughts and then my postgraduate research into depression, I found that lament had to form a crucial part of the Church's response to mental illness.

I felt then, as I do now, that only lament can hold the reality of the agonies of mental illness with the sovereign, all-loving and all-kind God. Lament is not only for those who are living with mental illness, however, it is a gift given to anyone so that they can call out to God when life hurts.

It was a long-standing joke between myself and my research supervisor that, having begun my research looking at suicide and progressing on to depression, I might end up doing a PhD on joy one day. While this is far from a PhD thesis, I have discovered that the path to joy is one paved with painful times and the way through these times is through lament in every season of life.

In the years since I graduated my life has changed completely; like many others, my twenties have been a time of landmark events: moving out of home, engagement, marriage, new jobs, pregnancy and parenthood. They have also been spent, for the most part, working with and for churches to change attitudes towards mental health. I founded the charity ThinkTwice at the age of twenty, with little idea of how the years which followed would see an exponential rise in mental illness. What began on a scribbled page of my diary developed into a charity which I led for the next decade, travelling the country to preach at churches, deliver training and develop campaigns to equip the Church to face what has been called 'a mental health crisis of epidemic proportions'.

Alongside the professional, there has been the undercurrent of my own mental illness that is often well managed, but waves of which will sometimes still sweep me off my feet. It is less dramatic than it once was, no longer forcing me to walk the wafer-thin line between life and death. This is the aftermath of severe mental illness, when it is chronic, largely manageable, but still with the power to drain hope and colour from my life and still shaping the way I look at the world and the way I relate to God.

This book is an invitation to explore the interconnectivity of lament and joy, the discovery that not only can we rarely have one without the other, but that finding a rhythm of lament in our lives is part of the pathway to joy. I have chosen to cover the liturgical seasons because they so clearly demonstrate the ebbs and flows we are to expect in the spiritual life. We begin with Advent (the beginning of the Church year) and end with the second period of Ordinary Time, which takes up the best part of the year from May to December. The six chapters can be read at any time, but it might be especially helpful as a book to guide you through Lent or Advent as together we explore the Scriptures and explore God's gift of lament to face up to our pain and difficulties, so that we may inhabit the joy he made us for.

I found myself writing about the seasons in this book the wrong way around – thinking about Advent and Christmas during a blisteringly hot summer and Easter as the snow fell. But as I did, I discovered a new richness to hearing the message in a time that seemed to jar with my surroundings, so I hope that whenever you find yourself in these pages, you might glimpse something of the God who is the author of joy and our sustainer through grief's laments.

At the end of each chapter there are some reflective questions that you can either use to guide your own response or to shape conversations in small groups, in person or online. There is also a psalm to read after each chapter to encourage you to explore them through all of life's seasons. The Psalms are our prayer book and they include references to almost every emotion you can think of; in reading a psalm or two with each chapter, I hope to show how we can bring our joys and sorrows to God in all we face.

Writing this book has been a crash course in joy and lament, but I hope that you will find it to be a gentle guide as we explore where God is in the best and worst of times.

1

Advent: waiting

I don't know about you, but I've always loved Advent: the anticipation, the dark streets adorned with decorations and churches glowing with candlelight.

As a child, one of the things I loved the most about it was getting to open the small cardboard door of my Advent calendar and letting the sweet chocolate melt on my tongue before the day swung into action. It was a moment that marked the period as special, and the only thing better than that chocolate–a-day were the days when, by some miracle, you'd missed the day before and you got a double portion. Am I right?!

Despite my love of Advent, I have to admit to being rather oblivious to any of its theological significance. For me (and probably many others) it was simply the weeks in the run-up to the big day – Christmas!

It wasn't until I was about fourteen that I began to understand the poignancy of Advent. Depression had begun to wash through my mind and the scent of mulled wine and pine needles jarred against my unhappiness.

Nothing will ever be the same again

At an outreach event my church was holding, the choir began to sing the Graham Kendrick song 'Nothing Will Ever Be the Same Again' from his *Rumours of Angels* album and the words, which spoke of everything changing on the night God came to earth as a baby felt not comforting, but condemning.

I felt despair settle on my shoulders; I'd been baptized as a believer on a sweltering summer day only eighteen months before, and since then life had got harder and harder. All of a sudden it occurred to me that the characters in the Christmas story experienced more hardship than was bearable.

I thought of Joseph, told that the woman he wanted to marry was pregnant and the baby wasn't his. I thought of Mary, so young to be a mother – the same age as I was then, if the scholars were correct – and the shame of her pregnancy, the weight of responsibility to be carrying the Son of God. I couldn't even conceive of pregnancy, raising a child, let alone to be told that my child would be God's son and that I was impregnated by the Holy Spirit.

Nothing was ever the same again for them, and from what I knew things had been pretty bleak from thereon in for Mary and Joseph as they fled Bethlehem, escaping Herod's murderous regime, raised Jesus, felt him grow away from them and ultimately saw him arrested and crucified.

If nothing was ever going to be the same again in my life, surely that meant I'd have to live with this heaviness, these tears, for ever?

I somehow carried that belief around with me for many years after that night. I lost any sense that Advent, while a time of waiting, was also a time of joy because I was blinded by my own pain and circumstances.

It wasn't until I was nineteen and at Bible college that I heard the song again and realized what it really meant. It was the annual Christmas concert and a different choir sang the song – and it seemed to mean something different altogether. I wonder if you've experienced that feeling? That hearing something familiar can change your understanding completely in a new setting?

This time I heard the words 'Nothing would ever be the same' and realized that it wasn't because I would always be hopeless or always struggling; but because Jesus came.

And in his coming, he wasn't going to make life perfect, but the knowledge of all he had been through would be the ultimate balm for our wounds. We would never be alone in the pain or abandoned to hopelessness because Jesus himself is our hope and that hope transforms our waiting.

Waiting

It was a wait that the Jewish community knew all too well. They had been waiting for their Messiah, for the coming of the king that prophets had foretold for centuries. Isaiah 9.2–7 describes the king and future the exiled Jews were waiting and hoping for. They had lost everything in the preceding years; the promised land they had fought for had slipped from their grasp once more and they were under foreign rule again far from home. Isaiah's words would have been renewed comfort for their bruised and battered dreams of a king, not only because of the words he spoke, but also because he was so sure of the hope he was proclaiming. It was written in the past tense as if the light had already dawned – even though they were in the depths of darkness.

> The people walking in darkness have seen a great light; on those living in the land of deep darkness a light has dawned. You have enlarged the nation and increased their joy; they rejoice before you as people rejoice at the harvest . . . For to us a child is born, to us a son is given, and the government will be on his shoulders. And he will be called Wonderful Counsellor, Mighty God, Everlasting Father, Prince of Peace. Of the greatness of his government and peace there will be no end.
> (Isaiah 9.2–3a, 6–7a)

I can imagine that they took great solace in Isaiah's certainty that their captivity would not last forever and that their new king would be everything they could have dreamed of in a ruler.

He was going to be a wonderful counsellor and the word counsel comes from the idea of being advised, but Jesus would be far more than a dispenser of good advice. In his humanity he experienced the whole spectrum of human emotions: from the brightest joy to the most desperate hopelessness in order to bring humanity and God together in a way no one would expect.

Not only that, but the coming king would be a mighty God. I don't know about you, but I can tend to think of Jesus at Advent only as a meek and mewling baby, far from the image I've also held of a herculean figure, physically strong and powerful. But Isaiah's words remind us of just what Jesus gave up to be Mary's son. He traded the throne of heaven for scratchy straw, the power of the cosmos for the weakness of a human baby. Jesus was not just going to be someone who could say 'I know how you feel'. Isaiah's prophecy tells us that we can cry out to our Saviour, not just because he understands our weaknesses, but because he can conquer them with his strength and power.

This wise and mighty king was also going to be an 'everlasting father'. Jesus' earthly ministry cared for the forgotten, the widow and the orphan. His priorities would come directly from the Father, whose power reigns forever. And in among the maelstrom of politics and fake news, in trusting Jesus, we aren't entrusting power to a corrupt politician or an adulation-seeking celebrity, but to the king who will reign forever, the only one deserving of worship and praise. His royalty is demonstrated in the gifts he is given by the Magi; the NIV tells us that they offered baby Jesus their treasures – but they also offered him gifts that marked him as a king. Gold, frankincense and myrrh were traditional gifts to bring before a monarch, but they also marked the path that Jesus would walk in his life and death: gold for a king, frankincense for a priest, myrrh to prepare for his life-saving death. The gifts also gave a message proclaiming what kind of king Jesus is: He is not a tyrant like Herod, only interested in his own agenda and power; he is loving and cares for his people, he will provide for them and he will offer himself again and again until he is emptied.

Lastly, he was going to be called Prince of Peace. The idea of a Prince of Peace can almost sound a bit wishy-washy; it can seem to be a vague concept more akin to the wishes of a Miss World candidate than a king (is it just me that cannot think about Miss World without also thinking about the noughties film *Miss Congeniality*!?)

But peace according to Sandra Bullock does the peace of Jesus a disservice. This is shalom: the wholeness of God which Jesus showed again and again during his earthly ministry as he healed the paralysed, forgave even the gravest sinners and died so that we might join in his righteousness. Shalom is the scent of the garden of Eden through security, well-being, hope, friendship and justice; we won't experience it in its fullness yet but we will catch the fragrance of it through relationships, community and the world around us.

This glorious promised leader was not going to come in the blaze of glory they expected. He was going to come from the darkness and the silence. It was, even then, an almost bittersweet promise because no one knew how long the wait would be. Advent reflects that: holding together the joy of the promise and the agony of the anticipation, the darkness waiting for the light. Biblical commentator Seitz writes, 'before we encounter a people who see a great light, we must first encounter a people thrust into thick darkness'.[1]

It's something which is reflected not only in human history, but in nature – when the darkest hour comes right before the dawn.

The darkest night

I love that Advent in England happens in the depths of winter; the nights are long and the decorations shine all the brighter as they adorn the cold and dreary streets. I can't imagine experiencing Advent in midsummer (although it would be nice to avoid the winter colds over the festive period!). But as December begins, the seasonal weather reflects something of what Advent teaches.

As Advent approaches its climax, in the northern hemisphere we mark the winter solstice, the darkest day of the year. Author Catherine McNeil notes:

> On the darkest day, during the longest night, we turn a corner . . . the light is coming, and though we see or feel nothing at all, what will be is certain and cannot be undone. Like so many victories it is silent 'already not yet'.[2]

The darkness is not just something to be feared; it's the sign of a pivot point – a new beginning which points us all the way back to the first beginning, where God spoke light and creation into the darkness.

I have sometimes wondered why, when God began his work of creation, he didn't just banish the darkness altogether. Instead he kept it, pulling it apart from the light but making it a part of the world he called 'good'. Perhaps the fact that life itself begins in the dark is a reminder to us that we need the darkness as much as we need the light?

My son was born right at the end of November into the darkest weeks of the year, and in his first weeks and months I saw the hours of darkness more than I ever had done before. There was something about those silent hours in the dead of night that had a kind of peace to them (apart from the cry of my newborn).

So often, darkness is demonized, isn't it? And yet the whole of creation needs it. We need the darkness of night as much as we need the light of day and many beautiful things have their beginnings in the darkness. As Barbara Taylor Brown writes in her gorgeous book *Learning to Walk in the Dark*, 'New life starts in the dark whether it is a seed in the ground, a baby in the womb, or Jesus in the tomb.'[3]

It seems obvious when you think about it: Jesus wasn't resurrected in the sunshine, but in the darkness of the tomb; Jacob's blessing comes with wrestling under the cover of darkness, not with ease in the sunshine. Flowers need the darkness of the ground to bloom and babies need the comforting darkness of the womb to grow before they face the light of the world.

Darkness wasn't created, it's an absence not a presence – but God didn't eliminate it from the creation he called 'good'. Perhaps it's because, as Psalm 139.12 recounts, 'even the darkness will not be dark to you; the night will shine like the day, for darkness is as light to you'.

So I wonder if it's time to rethink darkness, to consider the wonder and potential that it holds. My son has helped me with this; at two he is yet to fear the darkness and loves nothing more than getting us to switch the lights off and play with the risk of bumping into things and falling over (toddlers are strange and wonderful creatures!).

There is a mystery and wonder in the dark that is immediately dispelled when the lights come on. Advent seems to tell us that the dark is not all bad because the beginning of our long journey home began in the darkness and the silence; the journey to the light and joy of Christmas cannot be glimpsed without understanding how to work in the dark.

Something about Mary

Over the past few years, it has become almost impossible for me to separate Advent and motherhood, having both lost a baby and birthed a baby as the fairy lights first began to twinkle. And, of course, because of the central mother in the gospel story, Mary.

There is something extraordinarily ordinary about Mary, the least likely candidate to carry the Messiah. And yet she was a demonstration of the way God was going to enact the next chapter of his story – it would not be the rulers and warriors on the front line, but the poor, the forgotten and the broken.

Her significance is not just that she's an unlikely choice for mother of the Messiah, but also how she responds to the task God gives her with a willingness that I'm not sure I'd have been brave enough to show!

In Luke's Gospel we read about the pregnancy of Mary's cousin Elizabeth before we read about Mary's, and it's almost as miraculous. Elizabeth was an old woman when we meet her in the story, well past childbearing years, and yet much like Abram's wife Sarai before her, she falls pregnant in her twilight years. The parallels between Elizabeth and Sarai don't end there. Upon hearing about her own promised child, Sarai laughs, and when Elizabeth's husband, Zechariah, is visited by an angel to proclaim their late-in-life conception, he is so unbelieving that he's struck dumb at the news, unable to speak until he meets his baby who himself will break the 400 years of silence from God's prophets since Malachi.

It's Elizabeth whom Mary visits to come to terms with her own angelic visitation. But Mary's pregnancy was the opposite of longed for, wasn't it? Perhaps you're well-versed with the story of the virgin conceiving?

When I was ten, I played the role of Mary in my Year 6 nativity, complete with a costume of ill-fitting sheets and a doll to represent Jesus (if I recall correctly, the baby's head fell off a worrying number of times during the performances!). The chorus of my solo spoke of Mary's incredible obedience, 'Lord as you've spoken, let it be. May your will be known through me' and I remember even then being somewhat incredulous that the news of her pregnancy was adjusted to so easily. It's how the story is so often told, that Mary replied with simple, uncomplicated obedience. But in Paula Gooder's book, *The Meaning Is in the Waiting*, she notes that 'the Greek word dietarachthe means "deeply agitated"' – but more at the appearance of the angel than the news of the baby! Gooder goes on to explain that 'Mary's calling is that she understands that being favoured by God is as much to be feared as embraced'.[4] It's a familiar feeling when it comes to calling, isn't it? In my own life, any sense of calling has been as fearful as it has been exciting.

The fear that Mary experiences upon seeing the angel does not dissipate in the face of the news; I'm sure that her betrothal to Joseph and the fear of being stoned for adultery were thoughts not far from her mind, and yet she chooses obedience. She chooses the discomfort of pregnancy over the ease of a young woman's freedom, fear for her future ahead of the security her marriage to Joseph would offer.

And yet her obedience is rooted, not in a sense of heavy duty; but in her knowledge and delight of who God is. *The Message* translation puts the beginning of the Magnificat, Mary's song in Luke 1.46–55, in the following way:

> I'm bursting with God-news;
> I'm dancing the song of my Saviour God.
> God took one look at me and look what happened –
> I'm the most fortunate woman on earth!

What God has done for me will never be forgotten,
The God whose very name is holy, set apart from all
    others.

It's an exuberant offering of praise from a girl who knows and trusts the Lord and is, I think, meant to remind the reader of Hannah's prayer of thanks at the birth of Samuel, when she also declares her praises with singing and rejoicing. These are the songs of two mothers for their sons, and yet both would lose their sons.

Mary would stand at the cross of her son, watching him take his last breath.

Hannah would hand her son over to the care of Eli, who would raise him.

The bittersweet joy of these two mothers is perhaps echoed in the life of every mother. It's certainly been true in my own journey to motherhood. Having had Hannah's prayer recited over me as I lay in the Special Care Baby Unit (more in my book *Learning to Breathe*), when I discovered I was pregnant for the first time I offered the same prayer with joy and hope filling my heart. In the days that followed my husband and I planned where a cot would fit in our flat, how we would decorate the nursery, imagined who the baby would grow to be. But then the bleeding and the ache, the fear and frustration, as we were told little could be done on a snowy December weekend, that we must wait out the pain.

As it continued, I clung to the most fragile of hopes that this little baby (the size of a chocolate chip the app told us) would survive. The uncertainty was agony and as time went on I knew in my head that I was probably losing the baby, but I refused to believe it; there was hope. My husband and I huddled together and watched countless episodes of our favourite sitcom, pleading with God. All we could do was wait for Monday. As the weekend passed our prayers changed as our hope flickered falteringly, I just wanted to know what was happening. Our changed prayers were answered: no wait for an appointment, a scan that same day. In the small cramped room of the Early Pregnancy Unit, the screen showed starkly that our baby was gone.

The Advent that followed was excruciating; the message of the baby Jesus in his mother's arms as shepherds sang for joy. The miscarriage caused me to strip back to the basics of my faith, past the theological words and atonement theories to the truth that had captured my heart aged five. That God is our loving Father – and he won't leave us in the dark without his light.

In the midst of my grief, hanging on to the hope of the light was my sustenance. I would return time and again to Hannah's earlier, less triumphant prayer in the months that followed when I fell pregnant again and my son began to grow within me.

Advent and pregnancy, especially those final heavy months, seemed to have a lot in common and as the following Advent approached, along with my due date, I was drawn again to the paradox of it all. The darkness of the womb sustaining life; the baby I was carrying only possible because of the baby I'd lost.

The Carmelite community, whose origins can be traced back to hermits living in Mount Carmel where the prophet Elijah defeated the prophets of Baal, uses four themes throughout the weeks of Advent, different to those of the Church of England. The themes linger on waiting, accepting, journeying, and birthing and when I first came across them it occurred to me how much they encapsulated the experience of pregnancy. The waiting for each week to pass, each trimester to begin and end; the acceptance of a changing body, changing priorities; the journeying through the weeks full of hope and fear, before the birthing, which marks the end of pregnancy but the beginning of a fresh adventure.

Waiting

Advent presses the point that God's people are a waiting people. From Abram and Sarai waiting for the child who would bring the promised descendants, to Joseph waiting in his prison cell to be remembered by those he'd sought to help, to the Israelites desperate for freedom and a land to call home. These times of waiting, as with Advent, are a reminder that God works in our waiting, that they are not wasted times, but refining, hope-filled fire.

Accepting

It was the word accepting that captivated and confused me in equal measure. For me at least, it conjured the concept of

Elisabeth Kubler-Ross' famous five stages of grief: denial, anger, bargaining, depression and, at last, acceptance. It's the pinnacle stage in this model, whereby someone can see some kind of resolution to the pain of grief. Its place as the second week of Advent, then, feels strange. And yet, as I delved into the ancient stories again, both the gospel narratives and the story of the Carmelites, I began to see it a little differently. The Carmelites had been crusaders who'd gone to fight but ended up so transformed that they stayed to pray and build a community in the Holy Land.

It reminded me how often in the Scriptures God shows up in the most unexpected ways, calling unexpected people to do unexpected things. A virgin conceiving. A barren woman falling pregnant while her husband falls silent. When we agree to follow the way of Jesus, we agree to the unexpected. And sometimes, the unexpected way we are called to, hurts. It's all too easy to miss the trouble woven through the nativity, in Mary's distress, Joseph's confusion and Zechariah's silence. God does not hide from us the fact that the walk ahead with him is not easy. As Timothy Keller writes in his book *Hidden Christmas*: 'The manger at Christmas means that, if you live like Jesus, there won't be room for you in a lot of inns.'[5]

Journeying

The journeying is easier to see and I can't even begin to imagine how uncomfortable that journey to Bethlehem would have been on foot and by donkey for a heavily pregnant Mary. There's something about journeys that disrupt us and the carefully choreographed rhythms of our lives; perhaps it's that they signal change (something I'm not a great fan of) and, throughout history, God disrupts his people. He sends them to new places, on new adventures and asks us to take each step away from certainty and towards him. Perhaps the reason he speaks so loudly to us on journeys is because we are already distracted from day-to-day life. Advent retells Jesus' journey to be with us, one not done in majestic fashion, but one that began in the womb of a teenager and ended on a criminal's cross.

Jesus' journey to be with us is the greatest comfort in the darkness and ignited the flame of hope for evermore – it is what keeps me walking this strange journey of surrender and freedom. Malcolm Guite's beautiful poem 'O Emmanuel' captures something of the mystery of Jesus' journey to us as our hope, speaking of being enfolded into time and place, finding grace in a womb for our oh-so wounded world.[6]

Birthing

And then, at long last, the birthing. I read these words by the author Sarah Bessey, not long after I gave birth, and they were the most true thing I held on to in those early weeks. 'Birth is never not a miracle . . . It's never not the best and worst at the same time.'[7] Birth is the place where the threshold of life and death is the faintest line and I've been wondering what Mary's birth was like. We know there was no pain relief, that there was no shiny hospital or consultants on call. But was it long? Did she wonder if she could do it? Did she beg and plead for it to be over? (I'm guessing she didn't cry 'it's like the cruciatus curse!' like I did at some point between my waters breaking and being administered some very powerful medication.) The thing is, whichever way we look at it, birthing is painful.

> The seed breaking through the ground to the light. The baby breaking through to begin life in the outside world. The butterfly breaking through its cocoon to fly. The stars breaking through night's sky.

We can't separate birthing from breaking. But that also means we can't separate breaking from the beauty of joy. The pain of birth certainly felt like a breaking, if nothing else it was a breaking of my old life, but the new life was and is undoubtedly beautiful. All too often, we hold back from the birthing because we fear the breaking. We fear breaking ourselves open to allow God to do a deeper work; we fear breaking open new possibilities in case we fail.

The concept of birthing isn't limited to physical childbirth. Just reading that word may be like scraping a bruise; it might be the one thing you long for and it might be a distant dream. But it doesn't mean that there won't be new things breaking through the cracks of the pain, shooting through the darkness like a seed seeing the sun. It might be the journey to parenting relationships with godchildren, stepchildren or through adoption and fostering. It might be the breaking open of an idea, of seeing something so long worked on come into the light for others to see.

Advent is a season of waiting, accepting, journeying and birthing; it's almost as if we must come to terms with these things before we can fully move into the joy of Christmas. It is the same throughout the Christian year, as we will see. Before the jubilation and celebration of Christmas and Easter, we must work through the repentance and grief of Advent and Lent.

These are times of preparation, not unlike the period of engagement before marriage, or gardening leave between two jobs, where our waiting helps us to come to terms with a new beginning. We have to trust in the waiting as Elizabeth and Zechariah did, accept the part we're given in God's audacious plans, go on the journey of faith and fear along with Mary and Joseph and experience the agony of the birthing.

Questions for reflection

1 Do you think it's important to mark Advent? What traditions do you have or would you like to include in your home?
2 How does the darkness make you feel? Is it something you fear? Could you ask God to help you to find 'treasures in the darkness'?
3 Consider the times in your life which might have included the Carmelite themes of waiting, accepting, journeying and birthing. How have they changed your view of God?
4 Reflect on Psalm 139, perhaps use a journal or journalling Bible to focus on verses 11 and 12 which speak of 'darkness not being dark' to God.

2

Christmas: celebrating

Christmas.

It's a word that can conjure a hundred images isn't it? From the wonder in the face of a child upon seeing what Father Christmas has left, to a table creaking under the weight of a plump turkey, towers of potatoes and the debris of cracker toys. Almost all of the images (in my mind at least) are lit by the soft glow of candlelight and fairy lights, with people surrounded by those they love the most.

And yet, this is not a picture that rings true for everyone. Instead of happy family scenes there might be conflict and loneliness; longing and scarcity instead of plenty; the agonies of grief at the empty spaces around the table; just another day to battle through.

This was brought into sharp focus in 2020, with so many of us having Christmases far from our dreams. Instead of full tables, people sat miles away from their families, while still others were suited in personal protective equipment trying to save the lives of people ravaged by coronavirus and comforting those who could not have their loved ones beside them as they died.

My own Christmas was scaled back, but I felt perhaps more connected to the story of strangeness and alienation of the

Incarnation than ever before. In the quiet moments, without the usual noise and rush, I felt God come close. Amid the chaos and confusion, the reality of what Jesus relinquished for us when he swapped the heavens for the manger struck me afresh. As I trudged up the hill to an outdoor carol service after a rather fraught bedtime with my little boy, I was confronted with the strange reality that the Creator of heaven and earth came to earth, not just to stay a helpless baby, but to go through the seasons of life from stubborn toddler years to the realities of adult life. It is these lengths to which Jesus went for our sake that are our ultimate reason to celebrate.

Even in the most ordinary of years, Christmas is a time of heightened emotion, a time when we're expected to be happy and can feel the pressure to hide behind fake smiles instead of answer the season's greetings with honesty.

But it was never meant to be like that; Christmas has the rawest beginnings. There was little splendour in a baby laid in a manger, or shepherds cowering at the sight of angelic hosts and the baby boy who would be the greatest reason for joy the universe has ever seen.

Joy to the World

Christmas is a time to celebrate the joy of who Jesus is and the joy the incarnation brings. We sing 'Joy to the World', but I think we sometimes misunderstand what joy really is, don't we? We can be tricked into thinking that Jesus came to make us happy, to give us an easy life and when life is hard we rail at God that this wasn't part of the deal!

Particularly in the West, we use joy and happiness inter-changeably and so we've come to expect ease and comfort in life as a sign of our faith. The prosperity gospel shows up in our own theology in subtle ways. Author Kate Bowler, whose PhD looked at the American prosperity movement writes:

> I would love to report that what I found in the prosperity gospel was something so foreign and terrible to me that I was warned away, but what I discovered was both familiar and painfully sweet: the promise that I could curate my life, minimize my losses, and stand on my successes. And no matter how many times I rolled my eyes at the creed's outrageous certainties, I craved them just the same. I had my own prosperity gospel, a flowering weed grown in with all the rest.[1]

Perhaps you have your own prosperity gospel that you cling to; I know that I've tricked myself into believing that God owes me happiness, or that tithing entitles my family to a measure of financial comfort. It's the equivalent of a faith security blanket that ultimately leads to our faith being dependent on our circumstances, how hard we work or feelings of joy, instead of Jesus' saving work.

The prosperity gospel teaches a false joy, one dependent on material success and wealth. But the gospel of Jesus Christ teaches something altogether different – a joy dependent solely on God as the source and sustainer of our joy, through Jesus and his incarnation, by the power of the Holy Spirit.

Real joy doesn't seek to eliminate discomfort or pain, but faces it with honesty. In the Bible, we see a number of different words used to mean 'joy'. In the New Testament, words which represent joy occur 326 times, which is strange considering how much death and suffering is contained within its stories! Some of the more common expressions used are 'agalliasis' which represents exultant joy, 'euthymein' which is similar to optimism, 'makarios' which means blessed, and the most common, 'chara', meaning inward joy and rejoicing. They represent a whole spectrum of joyful feelings rooted in who God is and what he has done for his people.[2]

These words describe not just an emotional response or feeling but a quality of character, for example when Paul talks about the fruit of the Spirit in Galatians where joy sits among love and peace.

And it is Jesus who is our example in living with and in true joy. Jesus, the one called 'Man of Sorrows' was also a man of joy from beginning to end, not because his life was happy and easy (far from it) but because he remained connected to the source of all joy and encouraged his disciples to do the same.

In his words in John's Gospel, Jesus describes himself as the true vine. In John 15.1–4 he says:

> I am the true vine, and my Father is the gardener. He cuts off every branch in me that bears no fruit, while every branch that does bear fruit he prunes so that it will be even more fruitful. You are already clean because of

the word I have spoken to you. Remain in me, as I also remain in you. No branch can bear fruit by itself; it must remain in the vine. Neither can you bear fruit unless you remain in me.

Jesus is telling his disciples that there is no way to experience joy apart from himself, and the same is true for us today. We may each experience happiness and enjoyment of life, but joy only comes from being connected to the source – Jesus – and it happens regardless of circumstance. Keeping connected to Jesus is about cultivating practices and rhythms in our everyday lives which enable us to hear from God's word and speak to him in prayer and worship; that's what enables us to live joy-filled lives despite our circumstances.

Unexpected messengers

The news of the birth of Jesus was sent first to people as unexpected as Mary and Joseph. The image of the shepherds watching their flock beneath the stars is synonymous with Christmas, with small children draped in sheets herding toy sheep; but in reality it was dangerous work.

Jewish scholar, Alfred Edersheim, has highlighted that even though shepherds were often outcasts, and considered ceremonially unclean because they lived with sheep, those tending to the flocks near Bethlehem may have been looking after flocks which would be used as temple sacrifices, meaning that these were priests as well as shepherds. The Lord who is the shepherd, caring for lambs and walking with them through the most difficult terrain, was now coming as one of the lambs to be sacrificed.

And when the angels appear, they would again speak first with reassurance, just as they had done to Mary and Joseph. Luke 2.10–12 records:

> Do not be afraid. I bring you good news that will cause great joy for all the people. Today in the town of David a Saviour has been born to you; he is the Messiah, the Lord. This will be a sign to you: you will find a baby wrapped in cloths and lying in a manger.

The message from the angels for the shepherds was about to change their whole lives, with a message for the whole world. I love how, despite probably getting the fright of their lives when their usual evening routine was interrupted by a host of angels, the shepherds wasted no time in going to find out more, in wanting to see Jesus for themselves. What's more, verse 20 tells us that they became Jesus' first evangelists, telling everyone they knew about their encounter, praising God as they went. Jesus' interruption of their lives didn't lift them away from their difficulties, but brought his good news into their difficulties, and isn't the same true of us today?

Encounters with Jesus change everything – but not in the ways we might expect.

It was the same for the infant Jesus' meeting with the elderly Simeon and Anna when he was presented at the temple. The eighth day after his birth was a significant one; he was to be circumcised and given the name Jesus. Waiting at the temple for the little family were Simeon and Anna. This pair are 'Israel in miniature'[3] according to the commentator Fred Craddock: waiting for consolation and redemption with both the hope of joy and the pain of conviction, both of which will be found in this baby.

Simeon and Anna are faithful in waiting for the Messiah; Simeon has been promised the Messiah by the Spirit before his death and Anna was a widow who spent her days at the temple fasting and worshipping. They have both dedicated their lives to God and want to pray over and bless Jesus.

Simeon's words are full of the sharp paradox which characterized Jesus' life. Luke 2.34 tells us:

> This child is destined to cause the falling and rising of many in Israel, and to be a sign that will be spoken against, so that the thoughts of many hearts will be revealed. And a sword will pierce your own soul too.

These are powerfully prophetic words; as a sword will indeed pierce Jesus' side and Mary will grieve the loss of her firstborn, standing beside his cross as he breathed his last. Over two thousand years later it's an experience which anyone can imagine would have been the worst of her life. While Simeon's words point to Jesus' own future, Anna's look forward to how the people of God will be freed through him.

The last visitors Mary, Joseph and Jesus welcomed are the mysterious magi. In all likelihood, the magi probably didn't arrive on the scene until Jesus was a toddler and it's hard to imagine how the little family would have reacted when these strangers appeared at their door. Again, there are similarities with Abraham and Sarah's story that we saw earlier: three mysterious visitors appearing because a baby would be born to 'bless the nations'.

It isn't exactly clear who these magi were; 'magoi', as the Scriptures call them, can be translated as magician, members of a priestly caste or astrologers. But they were definitely Gentiles (non-Jews) and men educated in astronomy. Stargazing in the first century was not the preserve of a column in a women's magazine, but rather the work of dedicated and educated watchmen, trying to discern what God was saying through the stars and how they should respond. The fact that they were entrusted with the news of Jesus' birth was yet another sign that Jesus was coming for everyone, regardless of wealth, status or race. This is joy for everyone – not just the Israelites' descendants – God was widening the definition of what it means to be part of his family.

So when the magi discerned that this star was about the King of the Jews, they unsurprisingly headed straight for King Herod. They went looking for Jesus in the palace, but found him, perhaps no longer in the manger (what with him being a toddler) but somewhere humble, far from Herod's palatial pad.

We see the strangeness of Jesus through the gifts the magi brought the infant Jesus, not the most practical for a toddler, but gifts which pointed towards Jesus' future; the truth of his majesty alongside the agony that was to come. The gold to mark Jesus as a majestic king like his ancestor David, the myrrh – an oil that was used both to anoint and prepare a body for burial and the frankincense – a sign that Jesus was not just royalty but deity.

Herod is a dark figure, a bloodthirsty king who, unable to locate Jesus when the magi don't return to him, ordered the death of all infant boys. The infanticide is triggered by the birth of the one baby born to save others – it's the most heartbreaking paradox and one that means Jesus begins life as a refugee, far from heaven and far from his family home.

I love these words from Timothy Keller about the shadows of the Christmas story. He writes:

> Both secular and church celebrations of Christmas focus almost entirely on sweetness and light. They are all about how the coming of Christ means peace on earth . . . [but] the surgeon and the therapist often make you feel worse before you can feel better.[4]

He uses the example of the antiseptic, which stings as it cleans and heals – it's a paradox which runs not only through the Christmas story, but throughout our stories of faith in the suffering servant, fully God and fully human, who died so that we may have life.

I wonder if part of our problem with understanding joy (and how much the healing of God can hurt) is because we don't want to discourage people from bringing their lives to Christ. We want to tell the Christmas stories without also sharing the stories from the Advents and Lenten times in our lives when God is on the move in the darkness.

Healing or cure?

All over the world, there are things for sale to make life better. From the billion-pound wellness industry to rampant consumerism, we are a people in pursuit of happiness – and we want the Church to be a part of that. We want our evangelism to bring people into our churches, so we produce glossy videos to tell stories with happy endings and triumphant miracles.

We want to tell our gospel stories – how meeting Jesus has changed our lives – but we also need to be encouraging stories from the middle, of how we've met God even when our situations haven't changed. Stories of how we may not have been cured, but how we have experienced healing. While a cure may involve God removing something from you, healing centres on inviting God into your pain and brokenness.

The late author Rachel Held Evans wrote:

> There is a difference between curing and healing and I believe the church is called to the slow and difficult work of healing. We are called to enter into one another's pain, anoint it as holy and stick around no matter the outcome.[5]

It's a difference seen throughout Jesus' ministry; while he cured a number of people from conditions such as leprosy and bleeding, he offered healing to everyone he met by showing them the way to invite God into their places of pain and shame.

As we celebrate Christmas, we recognize that Jesus came to be with us in the dark times of life as well as the times of happiness and light.

Mother's treasure

As I've written, I've been drawn again and again to Mary: all that she went through from the societal shame to the rigours of pregnancy and birth. When she praised God in the Magnificat she knew she was beginning a difficult journey, but she worshipped in spite of it and throughout the Gospels we see how she responds to each new challenge and visitor. One of the most captivating verses about Mary for me is recorded in Luke 2.18 and 19, when her little family is visited by the shepherds, 'And all who heard it were amazed at what the shepherds said to them. But Mary treasured up all these things and pondered them in her heart.'

There's something wonderfully normal in her response to extraordinary circumstances, because mothers all over the world in all the ages have treasured the words given to them about their children.

Not long ago my little boy started at a childminder. Having been with us at home for four months during the lockdown, I was apprehensive about how he would cope, but slowly he began to show his childminder more and more of his personality until one day I got a text to tell me that he'd been chatting to himself, smiling and making everyone laugh all day. He was settled, and beginning to show these new faces the best of himself. The text made my heart swell in a way it had never done before; this was new parenting territory but as I felt the joy of people getting to know my son, I thought again of Mary treasuring and pondering the words about her own son.

Before becoming a parent I heard countless times about the rollercoaster it would be; the highest joys and the most devastating lows would characterize the journey I was about to embark on and they sit closer than I could have ever dreamed. And as my son grows, it feels as if the rollercoaster is gaining speed at an alarming rate! From the pride at seeing him master new animal sounds (side note, why do we teach children animal sounds? I can't remember a time, until becoming a mum, when I felt compelled to find out what noise a Narwhal makes!), to the frustration of trying to decipher what his furious points and tears are trying to communicate to me. It's a reminder, and one far from exclusive to motherhood, just how closely our joys and sorrows sit; but it's also a reminder to celebrate our joys and give thanks for them and for our sorrows.

The art of celebration

I'm a big fan of celebrations (and not just because I'm a big fan of presents!) because I believe that achievements and milestones need to be marked as much as losses need to be grieved. Christmas is a time, not to pretend that everything is fine, but to celebrate the reality of what God did for us when he sent Jesus to live and die for us.

I was challenged when reading Lucy Rycroft's book *Redeeming Advent* to ensure that I paid as much attention to the message my home gave at Christmas as I did to the aesthetic. It was a reminder that as lovely as my meticulously colour coordinated decorations are, what is more important is that people know why we're celebrating. Christmas for us isn't just about our family – it's about the family of God marking the coming of Jesus. So alongside the colour coordination, we used our little lightbox to proclaim the truths of Christmas; it's a small thing but I want people to know that we are celebrating Jesus coming to us as 'God with us' – not just the presents coming to us!

Abraham Heschel writes challengingly of celebration as he says: 'People of our time are losing the power of celebration. Instead of celebration we seek to be amused or entertained. Celebration is an active state, an act of expressing reverence or appreciation.'[6]

Christmas is our time to express reverence at the awesomeness of the king of heaven coming to make his home with us and appreciating all that he has done for us. Our Jewish forefathers knew a thing or two about celebration; throughout the Old Testament we see them come together to eat, dance and drink wine to rejoice in what God has done for them. Our celebrations aren't limited to Christmas, though, and we can express our devotion and thankfulness to God throughout the year; whether it be as we watch a sunset on holiday or give thanks for someone we love on their birthday, true celebration expresses how we feel about our relationships and the world God has given us.

When I asked people on social media how they best celebrated, most people replied that celebrations for them were about food and family. Celebrating around a table with friends and family is how significant events have been marked in communities for millennia – from the candles blown out on a birthday cake to champagne toasts on a wedding day – food and drink are ways of connecting and celebrating. In my own family, celebrations have always revolved around food, both my dad and auntie work in the hospitality trade and celebrations are marked with the best cuts of meat from suppliers and wine. In fact, when I was six instead of wanting a big party with my friends I decided that I wanted to have dinner at our favourite Italian restaurant! The best celebrations, however, were those hastily thrown together by my grandma, which involved her buying up the party food of a certain supermarket famed for caterpillar birthday cakes to provide a 'bitty tea' with sausage rolls, smoked salmon and canapés, meant for swish soirées. In my own house now, I'm the same and am in firm agreement with my grandma that celebrations should involve food from the aforementioned food shop!

And while the specific supermarket is optional, the importance of food in celebration in rooted in our Scriptures when special offerings and foodstuffs were presented to mark the most important occasions, from the Passover lamb to the fattened calf welcoming the prodigal home. Food represents not culinary expertise, but the preparation for celebration and the meeting of loved ones around the table to eat together, in times of plenty and in times of want.

Some of my friends have continued the Jewish tradition of a Friday night dinner, where attendance is non-negotiable for family and anyone extra is welcome. It's something I'd love to have in my own family as my son grows older: a weekly celebration which welcomes those around us and provides a focal point of the week where we can reconnect with God and one another.

The strange thing about losing the art of celebration is that we've not lost them from our calendars; there are countless consumer opportunities throughout the year including Christian festivals such as Christmas and Easter, saints' days, and historical celebrations such as Guy Fawkes Night. What we have lost, in so many cases, is our connection to the celebrations. We might buy nice decorations and gifts for the people we love, but that has somehow become separated from what it is we are celebrating.

Most often, the connection to celebration that is missing is our thanksgiving for the reason for the celebration. If we empty our celebrations of thanksgiving, we are left with a party with no heart. Contemplative Henri Nouwen writes, 'joy is rooted in gratitude ... [They] always go together'.[7] If this is the case then perhaps it's no wonder we've become disconnected from joy and celebration, it's because we've forgotten how to be thankful. So perhaps we need to reorientate ourselves to the giver of all good things.

Throughout the Christmas story, we are presented with the ultimate reason to celebrate – God leaving the majesty of heaven to live through human life from the cradle to the grave. So how might we ensure our celebrations leave no one in doubt about the reason we're feasting?

Questions for reflection

1 Do you think celebrations are an important part of life? Do you have any particular traditions around your celebrations?
2 Do you agree that we have lost the art of celebration? Think about how perhaps celebrations have changed over the last decade – are the changes mostly positive or negative?
3 Read and reflect on Psalm 100; what are the elements of celebration that are spoken about in this psalm? How can we ensure we are more intentional about including them in our Christmas celebrations?
4 How might you ensure that people know the true reason for your celebrations this Christmas?

3

Ordinary Time: grieving

I should probably admit that before joining the Church of England in 2013, I'd never even heard of Ordinary Time. I grew up as a Baptist and the concept of Christian seasons beyond Advent and Lent wasn't explored; but over the past few years I've grown to love the idea of these seasons between the seasons. Ordinary Time is a translation of the Latin *empus per annum* – which translates 'time through the year'. It traditionally celebrates that Christ is active throughout all the mystery of human life – even when there aren't any specific festivals to mark.

I find Ordinary Time comforting; it recognizes that God is as present in our day-to-day living, in our working and our resting as he is in the times we come together to celebrate the big festivals. There are two periods of Ordinary Time throughout the liturgical year – one between Christmas and Lent, the other lasting from after Pentecost to Advent. We live our lives mainly within Ordinary Time and in this book we are going to focus on grieving for this first period, before looking at what it really means to rejoice in all circumstances in the second period of Ordinary Time. I hope that we will see that both grieving and rejoicing are important parts of our everyday and not something to be avoided.

You may be as unfamiliar as I was with the liturgical seasons of the Church of England since I found myself to be what I could call an accidental (and occasionally reluctant) Anglican. But while the phrases I use throughout this book are borrowed from the Anglo-Catholic tradition, I think we are all aware that our lives go through seasons of hardship and joy, high drama and the humdrum, so I hope that whatever your tradition or denomination is, you find the naming of these seasons helpful.

Loss and limits

Grieving is often thought of only in terms of death. It's seen as normal to grieve when someone close to us dies, but less so when we are grieving other kinds of loss. And yet loss is unavoidable. Peter Scazzero, author of *Emotionally Healthy Spirituality* writes that 'limits are behind all loss'[1] and if this is true (which I think it is) then loss is woven right through the fabric of our lives. Whether that be from mourning death, facing challenges that illness or disability bring, the end of relationships, or navigating the changes that life presents us, we must learn to grieve our losses and lament them to God so that we are able to cherish what we do have.

It struck me recently that one of the reasons I hate change so much is that every change involves a loss – even changes that we welcome. Whether it be the loss of freedom that marriage and parenthood bring, or the loss of familiarity when we change our job or location, these are losses that have to be dealt with so that we are able to fully enjoy what comes next.

During the last few months, I have made the decision to leave the organization I founded a decade ago, which has formed so much of my identity and been a vehicle of redemption and a garment of praise exchanged for the ashes of my greatest pain. God was very clear with me (well I felt he was clear) that I was to leave not because of what was coming next, but in obedience. I have had to cleave my identity away from what I have worked on for a third of my life and return my identity to my Creator. I have grieved ThinkTwice, not because I feel leaving is wrong, but because I have loved it, invested in it and to leave it means a seismic change in the way I live my life.

This grief is not the same as that I've experienced from the agonies of mental illness, or when I have been bereaved; but it has been a strange and uncomfortable path to walk. It is not a way I would necessarily have chosen to walk, but it is one I feel is important.

We are all desperate for there to be a hierarchy of pain, to rate what hurts. But in truth, pain is pain. Whether it be stepping on a plug or breaking a leg – it hurts. The consequence and the impact are different, but knowing that someone else has a broken leg doesn't make stepping on a plug less painful!

If we allow it to, though, it can enlarge our compassion. Grieving can bring us to our knees in prayer and help us to recognize that we need to rejoice with those who rejoice and mourn with those who mourn. It can allow the pain which breaks our heart open to become an offering.

You may be thinking that this seems a bit extreme; do we really need to grieve after something as joyous as bringing a child home or a new job opportunity?

Rethinking grief

In order to answer, I think we need to rethink grief a little. In the world we live in, grief is seen as something private, experienced in the aftermath of a death. We (perhaps unconsciously) think that there should be a time when we 'get over' grief and are able to live normally once more. Within our churches, we may rush to provide meals to the bereaved in the immediate aftermath of loss, but after the funeral we tend to believe that support is less needed.

Historically, however, grief and mourning lasted far past the funeral and had recognizable stages and practices. Queen Victoria famously wore black for 40 years until her own death after her husband, Prince Albert, died. Celtic grief practices include 'keening' – a loud wailing for the dead which gave voice to the internal grief. The Jewish culture has set rituals including three separate states of mourning, one before burial, then sitting 'Shiv'ah' for a week before a 30-day period of mourning.

In Job 2.11–13, we see Job joined by his friends Eliphaz, Bildad and Zophar, as he mourned the loss of his family and, in contrast to their later, less than helpful responses to Job's pain, here they simply came alongside him and 'sat Shiv'ah'. Shiv'ah allows a community to come around the grieving and join them without any expectation of 'cheering up' or moving on until they have begun to come to terms with what has been lost.

Throughout Scripture we see rhythms of grieving for the people of God – and it isn't limited to the death of loved ones. Prophets like Jeremiah weep and grieve over the message they have to convey and the exiled Israelites express their grief over the loss of their home, the promised land.

One such prophet was Nehemiah, who we meet in an interesting period in Israel's history. Originally the books of Ezra and Nehemiah were just one book, documenting the rebuilding of the temple for the Israelites who had returned to their homeland after exile in Babylon. Some have even called it Israel's second exodus, escaping captivity to return to their promised land. But for both exoduses their home, their promised land, was somewhere totally alien to them.

I should probably explain a little bit about the wall, because much of the weeping and grieving that goes on in the book of Nehemiah is about a wall – and I won't lie, it's taken me a while to get my head around this level of grief for a wall. But this wall meant far more to the people of Israel than just a piece of MDF between rooms. This wall was one which was meant to protect the city – the dwelling place of God for the people of God – and without it, it would have been vulnerable to attack or destruction, all the things they'd fled from. So Nehemiah's grief over a wall that he'd never even seen makes a little more sense because it represented the protection of his people.

It's easy to understand grief when it involves the death of someone we love, isn't it? There are rhythms and expected rituals to accompany that kind of grief – but the truth is not all grief involves bereavement. We need to grieve all our losses – whether it be the loss of a person, a place, a position or a system.

For some of us, grieving is something to be done in private and reading my words might feel uncomfortable, it might even feel a bit self-indulgent. But I'd ask that you bear with me, because I believe that now, more than ever, it's time for the church and wider society to grieve its losses before we can look forward to what we want to rebuild.

I'm sure many of you will be familiar with Elisabeth Kubler Ross' five stages of grief that I mentioned earlier in this book: denial, anger, bargaining, depression and acceptance have become common parlance in conversations about grief. But in fact, her stages were written about the journey of someone facing their own mortality observed through her work in hospices, rather than one for those who are left behind by grief. So I'm going to use William Worden's 'Four Tasks of Loss', which include accepting the reality, processing the pain, adjusting to the world and finding enduring connection, because, as I've delved into them, I've seen something of these tasks reflected in Nehemiah's grief and story.

Accepting the reality

Loss and grief don't work to a timetable; there is no predictability, but I do think there are paths to travel if we are going to learn to live with our losses. And the first of these is accepting the reality. For Nehemiah, this means that, although no longer in exile, the Israelites' promised land doesn't look how they expected it to; it's not protected and its people are 'in trouble and disgrace'. For all the years in exile, the Israelites would have looked back in nostalgia at their time inhabiting the promised land and looked forward to what it might look like to be home again. But the reality was that each stage of life and freedom offered up a new challenge – for some 'returning home' meant leaving everything they knew behind.

The acceptance also involved accepting the role Israel had to play in its own downfall. It was their sin that led to it taking 40 years to reach the promised land, and their repeated sins that led to their exile. And we have to accept the reality that it is the sin of the world (including our own) which means this world doesn't look like Eden – and it won't until Jesus comes again.

We need to weave repentance into the fabric of our prayer lives, not just for the things that we do wrong, but for the systemic wrongs of our world which amplify suffering, whether that be the systems which keep the poor poor, but enable our own social mobility, or the day–to–day stuff that causes grief to ourselves and others. In accepting the reality, we need to repent of our roles in the reality.

I don't know about you, but I have an idealized concept of what the world might look like 'post-COVID', one where we are able to take some of the rhythms we've learned in lockdown and apply them to normal life, that we won't take the simple pleasures of a meal with friends for granted – but I fear that I need to accept two realities. The first being that we don't know if, when and how the world will be 'post-COVID' and the second being that while we can all make personal changes, the problems of consumerism and loneliness will not disappear. The reality will not match the dream – but that doesn't mean all hope is lost.

Accepting the reality of our present isn't just about accepting the bad stuff – it's also about reaching out to Jesus, laying it before him and allowing ourselves to experience the forgiveness offered to us. Jesus did not just take the capital letter sins to the cross – murder, adultery, lying – but also our complicity. Nehemiah is our example, he prayed: 'I confess the sins we Israelites, including myself and my father's family have committed against you' (Nehemiah 1.6). It is an appeal to the mercy of God – and we are met there.

Processing the pain

When we accept the realities of our lives – whether it be the breakdown of a marriage, the loss of a job we love, or the separation of death – we are able to present them to God, to repent of the part we've played in wrongdoing and to lay our losses before him. And as we lay our losses before God, we have to process the pain. Nehemiah 1.4 tells us that on hearing about the broken walls of Jerusalem, Nehemiah weeps and mourns.

It can be tempting to read the Bible and conclude that there is something wrong with grieving. How many of us have heard 'don't grieve – just have hope' or 'the joy of the Lord is your strength' in the face of our own weeping?

For more years than I care to count, I only really knew one verse from the book of Nehemiah, and I used it as a stick to beat myself with. Nehemiah 8.10 says, 'Do not grieve, for the joy of the LORD is your strength.' For a long time, I really struggled with this verse; I thought it meant that being sad or grieving was a sign I was a 'bad Christian'. I wanted to bring people to Jesus – and I thought my own depression and tears would prevent that as I wasn't joyful. The words felt like a rebuke, telling me that there was no place for tears and pain in my faith. I don't actually remember ever being explicitly told these things, but it was reflected in the stories we heard in our church and in the wider evangelistic narratives of the time.

I heard stories from friends who became Christians at summer festivals and faith seemed to be the answer to their problems; but I felt like the older brother in the parable of the prodigal son. I'd been a Christian for over a decade at this point, but I was still crying, still struggling with depression.

In the years since, however, I've come to see, in the words of Timothy Keller, that 'sometimes the joy of the Lord happens inside the sorrow',[2] and Nehemiah's words here were specifically to those who, upon hearing the law read aloud, were beating themselves up and not wanting to enjoy the celebration of the new wall and all that it offered them. It wasn't a command never to grieve – it was a reminder of how much there was to celebrate for this particular people! I guess it's akin to us not moving from Lent to Easter – choosing to ruminate on our sin as opposed to rejoicing in the saving grace of Jesus. Paul gives a similar instruction to the Thessalonians: 'do not grieve like those without hope'; it's not an order never to grieve, but rather to grieve differently, to grieve as Jesus did.

Peter Scazzero writes, 'Jesus wept as one with hope, but his hope did not diminish his weeping.'[3] This is the great challenge for us I think – to grieve our losses while holding on to the hope of Jesus; but I think we see a little what that might look like from Nehemiah.

The reality is Nehemiah does a lot of weeping – in fact it's estimated that he wept and grieved for Jerusalem's walls for four months – and he'd never even been to Jerusalem! But more importantly, he brought his grief before God. The text tells us that he weeps, mourns, fasts and prays – he laments that which has been destroyed.

Author Mark Yaconelli writes: 'If I were to name the suffering that exists in the West, it is ungrieved grief. It is an unwillingness to admit, to name, to embrace the pain of life.'[4]

I've often wondered if grief is a little like a muscle, that we learn to grieve the little losses to equip us to face the world-shaking ones. We grieve the breakdown of our puppy love – and it feels as raw and painful as anything we've ever experienced – but getting through it allows us to see that we can survive. We grieve the adjustment of leaving home – and it prepares us for the millions of transitions and changes that life will throw at us.

So often, the problems arise when we are faced with insurmountable grief which collides with every other loss we've ever experienced and we find ourselves unable to cope with a thousand little losses, alongside the one that's changed our world.

Author Mags Duggan writes in her book, *God Among the Ruins*: 'I wonder if we sometimes miss how God might want to minister to us because we are too eager to move on, too quick to relieve the ache we feel with the analgesic of activity.'[5]

The analgesic of activity allows us to numb and ignore our losses and continue with our productivity, but it leaves us unable to hear what God is saying to us in and through our pain. Allowing ourselves to participate in the rhythms of grief and joy on the other hand enables us to be open to how God is moving.

Perhaps that's why we are called to 'weep with those who weep and rejoice with those who rejoice'. We do it again and again, not that it will become easier, but so that we will not lose ourselves in our grief, but join together as a community to bring the spectrum of emotions to God. We can rejoice for ourselves and those we agree with, but weep for those who are grieving, who do feel a loss.

Throughout the Church year, we are offered opportunities to grieve: whether it be alongside Mary as she adjusts to how her whole world changes as she carries the Son of God and is forced to flee in the night, as a refugee with her little family, from everything she's ever known, or as we walk the long road of Lent and Holy Week, facing our sin and our grief on the path to Calvary through the broken jar of perfume, the sweat-tinged with blood and the cries of 'Father forgive'.

Ultimately, we cannot avoid the pain and the struggle. We have to go through it. It's the sentiment of the children's book *We're Going on a Bear Hunt* – we cannot go around it, under it or over it, we must go through it.

Adjusting to the world

We do emerge from the intensity of early grief, just as Nehemiah does, and as we do so we have to adjust to the world. Nehemiah's adjustment begins in his prayer where he anchors himself to God, 'the great and awesome God, who keeps his covenant of love' (Nehemiah 1.5).

We too need our anchor in the unchanging character of God as we adjust to the world in which we're still grieving. We can process the pain of our losses in the presence of the God who loves us before we try to adjust to what the world now looks like for us.

Loss changes us and adjusts our vision – and that takes a period of adjustment. Philosopher Nicholas Wolterstorff writes in his book *Lament for a Son* after his son dies in early adulthood, 'I shall look at the world through tears. Perhaps I shall see things that dry-eyed I could not see.'[6]

It is one of the greatest mysteries of grieving that we receive something as we adapt to what we have lost. It's not something we would ever ask for or want, but perhaps it is a gift of grace.

Moving forward a little in the text to the start of chapter 2, Nehemiah approaches his boss and the text says, 'I had not been sad in his presence before, so the king asked me, "Why does your face look so sad when you are not ill? This can be nothing but sadness of the heart."'

I love this bit of tenderness that the king shows; I can only imagine that it's a bit like going to meet the Queen and her talking about the fact that you look sad. It's an almost outrageous show of humanity. It shows, I think, that Nehemiah is adjusting to the loss, he's able to be honest about his feelings, but he's also able to resume his work; that doesn't mean it's not hurting him, but it's the part of grief when life begins to resume in some way, shape or form.

Finding connection

One of the best quotes I've heard about grief is that it never gets smaller, but life gets bigger around it – and I think that comes from how we adjust to the world.

Perhaps the raw edges of grief have been smoothed a little, but it requires community. In the children's nursery rhyme

'Humpty Dumpty sat on a wall' that I was saying with my son recently, it struck me that it's pretty depressing!

Humpty Dumpty sat on a wall,
Humpty Dumpty had a great fall;
All the king's horses and all the king's men
Couldn't put Humpty together again.

The imagery which accompanies this rhyme is usually an egg sitting atop a wall, the egg falls and breaks and armies come to his assistance, but they can't repair Humpty and we leave the story there with a broken Humpty and the king's men and their horses left helpless.

Apparently it first appeared in print in 1797[7] and the poem meant to make the point that even the most powerful in society couldn't fix what was broken, but I can see here that something has changed – he's no longer alone. Humpty doesn't get put back together the way he was, but he has a community around him and that is a gift we can give one another as we grieve, to come alongside one another.

And as community we have to survey the damage and accept the new landscape of our lives before we can begin rebuilding. It's something we all have to do at times of change and upheaval, to accept what's been lost, grieve it and then think about how we can rebuild.

Rebuilding is harder than building, isn't it? I guess it's a little like lockdown – simple to enter into, but much harder to emerge from.

But what Nehemiah teaches us is that we need prayer and we need community to help us adjust to the new world we're living in. We need to be honest – with God and with those around us. It's a vital challenge so that others can help us navigate the new world we're living in.

It was a challenge for Nehemiah and his people – but it was also a challenge for Jesus' disciples. They'd walked alongside him, done life with him intensely for three years. They'd experienced together the loss of leaving their lives behind to follow Jesus, the challenges of trying to understand what he was saying to them, the trauma of his death and resurrection, then again as he ascended to heaven.

It was a loss, but it was one filled with hope because they were given this new way to connect with Jesus, and it's one we all share. The Holy Spirit.

At the end of the Gospels, we're introduced to this new way of relating to Jesus – a way that will last until he joins us again. Matthew 28.20 encourages the disciples that 'surely I am with you always, to the very end of the age'.

The question is, as author Beth Allen Slevcove writes, 'How can I honour the reality of brokenness without losing the memory and hope of wholeness?'[8]

The answer, I believe, is found through connecting to the one who is our hope of wholeness. Nehemiah's prayer echoes this, I think, grieving but holding on to the belief that the rebuilding will come and something will be made beautiful from the ashes of loss. It is what countless psalms do – grieve with hope.

Songs of Ascent

In the Psalms, there is a section called the 'Songs of Ascent', so named because the Israelites were looking up to God for help and comfort. It's believed that these songs were written by the exiles upon their return to the promised land, tasked with rebuilding the temple. The songs look back to what God has already done for them, how he has delivered them, as well as bringing their grief and tears before him. I think this is how we grieve with hope – by looking back to what God has done, as well as facing the reality of our present grief.

Psalm 126 is a model of this, particularly verses 3–6:

> The LORD has done great things for us,
> and we are filled with joy.
> Restore our fortunes, LORD, like streams in the
>   Negev.
> Those who sow with tears will reap with songs of joy.
> Those who go out weeping, carrying seed to sow,
> will return with songs of joy, carrying sheaves with
>   them.

There are, perhaps inevitably, quite a lot of harvest metaphors in this psalm, unsurprising as it's the work that so many would have participated in, but more unfamiliar to a millennial eye.

What is clear though is that facing our grief can and should be done before our Creator; we see this countless times throughout Scripture, that God can handle us expressing the depths of our pain.

More than this though, grieving with hope relies on our past experiences with God. We don't merely need to imagine that God is there, we are reminded to look back at all that he has already done, both for us individually and for others. I don't know about you but, when I was in my teens, one of the most popular poems shared around on bookmarks and notebooks was the Footprints[9] poem. No one is really sure who wrote it, but it recounts the journey of a man walking along a beach with God at the end of his life and looking back at the sets of footprints in the sand. At some points there are two sets, but as he looks back at the most difficult parts of his life, there is only one set. He assumes that it's because God left him when the going got tough, when the reality was that during those hardest of times he was carried by God, leaving only one set of footprints.

I remember being given numerous copies of the poem as I struggled with God about where he was in the midst of my depression; the message was the same from everyone – God has not abandoned you, look how far he has brought you. It was a comforting message then, and it still is, but I think there is further to go.

The comfort that God gives when we are grieving is not just that he looks after us, but that he has consistently looked after his people since the beginning of time. From clothing Adam and Eve, despite them having to leave Eden, to the countless times he calls the Israelite people back to himself when they yet again seek their gods elsewhere. We are not alone in hoping and waiting for God to show up and history shows us that he does so every time. It's why the Bible helps us to grieve with hope, because it records all the hopeless souls who have cried out to him and found God met them in their distress.

Verse 2 of Psalm 126, which talks about God 'restoring our fortunes', can again sound a little alien to our ears, but it's another encouragement to look back at what God has already done so that we may wait and hope for his help in the present.

And then we reach the section which sounds like a chorus: sowing tears and reaping joy. It is impossible to separate sowing and reaping: if you want to reap (get the end product) you have to first sow the seeds. But I wonder if we have so distanced ourselves from the process of creation that we forget it more easily than those who first heard this psalm?

We no longer need to plant and harvest our own crops, simply to pop to the supermarket. We don't necessarily have to eat what's in season – whatever flavours take our fancy can be delivered to us with the click of a button. So the idea that we must first sow tears before we can experience joy is equally mysterious to us. More often than not, rather than sowing our tears, we stem them and distract them away. We avoid grieving our losses and then wonder why joy seems so elusive.

The joy of returning with arms full of harvest, grown from our tears, is impossible to match and yet we miss it because we skip the tears in favour of the anaesthetic of work, hurry or distraction.

You might be feeling as though there is nothing you need to grieve, and that's great! But the call to 'rejoice with those who rejoice, and weep with those who weep' doesn't give us the option of opting out of grief because we aren't personally affected. If 2020 taught us anything, it's hopefully that community matters, that we can't act just for ourselves. We might not personally know anyone who worked for the NHS – but still we clapped together for our carers. We might have escaped losing anyone we love from coronavirus – but still we must come alongside those who did and remember those who lost their lives.

There is much to grieve in this world far from Eden, far from home. But we grieve with the hope of home, of heaven – and Scripture shows us how – through the art of lament.

Questions for reflection

1 What do you think of the phrase 'limits are behind all loss'? Have you experienced grief as the result of a limit that has cost you something?
2 How did you find you related to William Worden's four tasks of grief through your own losses?
3 How might we bring our 'little losses' to God? Consider using a passage from the Book of Common Prayer or something similar to find language for grief that you can use in your own prayer life or journal.

4 If you're grieving the loss of a loved one, write a funeral style tribute for them and offer it to God as a prayer for them and for the relationship you shared with them.

5 What might it mean in your setting to weep with those who weep and rejoice with those who rejoice? Perhaps offering companionship to someone bereaved or celebrating with someone who has completed a project important to them?

6 Read through Psalm 23 highlighting the characteristics of God that can provide comfort.

4

Lent: lamenting

Once a year, my social media goes from pictures of perfectly piled up pancakes to foreheads marked with dark smudges in a period less than 24 hours. On Ash Wednesday 2021, the Church of England even produced an 'ashed' Instagram filter so that people could participate without being in church due to the national lockdown. Shrove Tuesday and Ash Wednesday sit together in stark contrast to one another: a celebration of plenty alongside our corporate cry of desperation and need for God.

Ash Wednesday is a day for the rawest honesty about who we are, how we've failed and how much we are still loved. It is a day which marks the beginning of Lent, 40 days (excluding Sundays) before Easter Sunday which remembers the 40 days and nights that Jesus spent being tested in the wilderness before he began his public ministry. The practice of the ashing is found first in the book of Ezekiel 9.4 which describes a mark on the foreheads of those who 'grieve and lament over all the detestable things', and is a reminder that the book of Genesis tells us that we are formed from the dust. It's a theologically rich act which presents the story of our identity as beloved creations of God who have sinned and been sinned against. It is an act of repentance that tethers us to our Creator.

During Ash Wednesday services, the Scripture used is often from Joel 2 and the phrase from verse 13, 'rend your heart and not your garments', rings through churches at this time. I probably haven't really considered it much before now, because what does that really mean, to rend your heart?

Rending and repentance

The word 'rend' literally means to 'tear something into pieces', to 'separate into parts with violence'. This is not gently pulling away from something – it's not me peeling myself away from my sleeping son to rest him in his cot; it's pushing something as far away from myself as possible, making sure every connection is broken.

Joel 2 is a call for God's people to return to him in repentance – not to just make a show of repentance for the eyes of the world by tearing their clothes, but to realize the gravity of their sin in a way which breaks their hearts wide open allowing God to fill the broken places. At the heart of Joel's call to repentance is a reminder of the character of God who doesn't demand our repentance out of malevolence, but because he is 'gracious and compassionate, slow to anger and abounding in love' (Psalm 103.8).

Returning to God is not about coming to him cowed by shame – it's returning to the God who is grace, compassion and love. We see it most clearly in the parable of the prodigal son. He is ready to return, full of repentance, recognizing his wrongs, to take the place of a servant in his father's house; instead we see an extravagant display of forgiveness and love. Luke 15.20 says, 'But while he was still a long way off, his father saw him and was filled with compassion for him; he ran to his son, threw his arms around him and kissed him.' The extravagance of the son's sinful living is met tenfold by the extravagance of the father's love and joy at being reunited with his son. We might have these times of returning to God throughout the year, when we repent and re-connect. It might be during communion services at church, or among friends, but it's important to recognize that we need not wait for the specific season of the year to bring ourselves to God in repentance and lamentation.

The marking with ashes once a year means we are reminded of sin in a tangible way: the reality of our broken world, our broken relationships, our broken hearts. It is also a reminder to look forward, however, to what God does with broken people and broken things. This is not a season to be rushed – we must wait awhile in the dust, recognizing the pain we cause, the pain we are in; but it's never a hopeless pain and it points us forward to being reunited with the Father and celebrating his love for us – even when we get things wrong.

Lament is vital – but it's not the end of the story.

Season of lament

Lent is a season of lament and hope is found, as ever, not in the things we can do to fix ourselves or the world around us, but in our God who fills our broken places with himself. The rend-ing can be painful, but the glory comes in what God does in those broken places. The Japanese call this 'kintsugi' – where broken spaces are filled with gold and made all the more beautiful in those broken places.

Lament is one of those strange words which means a great deal to people of faith, but perhaps less to those unfamiliar with the Judeo-Christian faith. Lament is in the cracks of humanity's brokenness –it is a gift that we can bring our grief, rage and despair before God.

J. Todd Billings, a theologian who lives with incurable cancer, wrote in his book *Rejoicing in Lament* that 'We only fully enter lament when we realise that we're not just expressing ourselves to a human observer but bringing our burdens before the Lord, the Creator, the Almighty who – in light of our distress – is our Deliverer'.[1]

Lament expresses our need for relief and deliverance, while also trusting that God can and will work in us and in our situation. It's what makes lament distinct from moans, cries and frustration that we express to one another (most days!) – our friends aren't sovereign, our expressions aren't acts of worship, whereas our laments to God put him in his rightful place on the throne.

Lament is found throughout Scripture, but most notably in 40 per cent of the Psalms and (unsurprisingly) the book of Lamentations. Written in the wake of the Babylonians destroying Jerusalem, the five chapters, which serve as five songs/poems, call out to God, mourning that they have thrown away their homeland and their closeness with God because of their disobedience. The story of these times is found in 2 Kings and

Jeremiah 52, while Lamentations records the raw agony of God's exiled people, and in doing so gives us a pattern for our own mourning and lament.

For the writer of Lamentations (sometimes thought of as Jeremiah, also known as the 'weeping prophet'), the world has ended and the Israelites are left to survey the rubble the destruction has caused and, as we saw in Nehemiah in the last chapter, the grieving has to come before the rebuilding.

It was written during the biggest crisis the Israelites had faced in their living memory – much like the coronavirus has been for our generation – with everything that had been at the centre of their lives, and all the things they believed to be their birthrights (the temple, Davidic throne and the promised land), taken away from them. And before they could begin to rebuild their lives and corporate identity, they grieved.

When it was written in the original Hebrew, the five poems were acrostic, that is, every line began with the letters of the Hebrew alphabet, demonstrating in structure as well as content the totality of their grief and providing a comprehensive guide to the path of lament through it.

How to lament

The writer of Lamentations works through four themes in these poems: grief, complaint, anger and fidelity to God. If Nehemiah gives us permission to grieve, Lamentations shows us how to lament our grief in the presence of

God – demonstrating how to rage at him for all that has been lost without censure but not rejecting their fidelity to God.

The grief of Jerusalem is personified throughout Lamentations as the 'Daughter of Zion' and gives us a language for our pain and lament like no other. Being able to articulate our pain is important because when we are unable to put it into words it tends to spill out in less helpful (and arguably more painful) ways.

It's a lesson I've learned and relearned countless times throughout my life. Expressing our emotions comes so naturally to us as children (or at least it does to my child!). He can accurately express, with great volume, his joy, exhaustion, hunger, sadness and disgust – but helping him to articulate these huge feelings in a helpful way is considerably trickier.

Throughout Holy Week we see the themes in Lamentations reflected in Jesus' final days. He laments in complaint as he weeps over his city; shows his anger at the injustice in the temple courts; shows his fidelity to his friends – even as they betray him, and mourns in grief in the garden of Gethsemane the night before he is crucified.

At the centre of the book of Lamentations, there is one passage that is most often quoted. Lamentations 3.21–23 proclaims:

Yet this I call to mind
    and therefore I have hope:
Because of the Lord's great love we are not consumed,
    for his compassions never fail.

They are new every morning;
> great is your faithfulness.

It's pretty much the only bright spot in the whole book of Lamentations. The tiny word 'yet' changes everything; it's the pivot point of laments throughout Scripture when the reality of pain meets the power of God to move. Michael Card notes that the turning point is only available because of God's hesed, his loving kindness. He writes: 'hesed appears at this turning point. It marks the transition from despair to hope, from emptiness to a new possibility of becoming filled once more.'[2]

Yet

'Yet' changes everything, not just because it's a change of direction, but because it is a reminder that our situations, our pains, are not final. God meets us in them with his loving kindness and lament is the narrow road we walk which holds our faith, our pain and God's goodness in the unlikeliest alliance.

One example of this is Psalm 42, a song of lament which pivots on 'yet'. It starts with the psalmist presenting God with complaint and grief, but halfway through changes direction from how the psalmist is hurting to who God is and a redirection of the psalmist's soul heavenward. Verse 5 says: 'Why, my soul, are you downcast? Why so disturbed within me? Put your hope in God, for I will yet praise him, my Saviour and my God.'

We can assume there is no change in the psalmist's situation as the psalm progresses, but the focus moves from the writer's own pain and problem to remembering who God is and the power of his loving kindness. This is the pattern and power of lament which may not change a situation but radically alters perspective.

When I was a teenager and in the depths of depression, the chaplain of my school used an example of a bus and a mountain. When we are right up close to the bus, it fills our vision, blocking the mountain. We cannot envision what is beyond it but when we step back the bus doesn't change size but our vision is expanded and we can see what is beyond us, in this case, the might and majesty of a mountain. This is one of the ways lament works; it may not change our situation but it does enlarge our vision so that we are able to gain some perspective.

Complaint

Jesus was welcomed into the city like a king and yet he chose a donkey. The crowds cried 'save me' and then called 'crucify'. They thought they were witnessing the beginning of a political revolution, a plot to overthrow Roman rule. They didn't understand that Jesus was coming to offer himself as the lamb that was slain. Their king was not a warrior, but a weeping servant.

As he approached his destination, perhaps as the hosannas were still ringing in his ears, he wept. He wept because he knew what was coming for his city; he knew that in rejecting him, they were rejecting peace. He wept because he knew he was facing rejection and crucifixion. Two thousand years later, Jesus' tears for his city have become our tears for our cities. When I look at our cities, I can feel tears prick my own eyes. The way of peace is not being chosen.

For so many fear-filled people, the answer seems to be to make others fearful. Fear of knives leads people to arm themselves. In the year ending March 2020, there were a staggering 46,000 offences involving knives, and it is right that the Church is at the forefront of lamenting to God and driving change. Organizations such as Power the Fight, aim to 'empower communities to end youth violence' and demonstrate lament by complaint in action through educating young people and working with the government to enact change.

Complaint against God through lament is not a denial of God, however, it's testament to a relationship with him that we are able to be totally honest with him. Only in our most secure relationships, when we feel most loved, do we feel able to present our complaints. The Israelites were brutally honest with God about the big and the small things they were facing, from being fed up with the unvaried diet of manna to feeling abandoned as they waited desperately to reach the promised land.

Perhaps the most famous complaint came from the lips of Jonah when he was told to minister to the sinful Ninevites; he famously fled and found himself in the belly of a fish before ending up on the very mission he'd run from. After the mission we see Jonah complaining to God – not because of something against his character – but because of the very essence of his character, his grace and compassion. Jonah 4.2–3 recounts these words:

> Isn't this what I said, LORD, when I was still at home? That is what I tried to forestall by fleeing to Tarshish. I knew that you are a gracious and compassionate God, slow to anger and abounding in love, a God who relents from sending calamity. Now, LORD, take away my life, for it is better for me to die than to live.

It's the strangest lament, but it's seen again in the story of the prodigal son where the elder brother rages at the grace shown to his little brother. Even the most unjust laments are heard by God and absorbed and righted by Jesus.

Timothy Keller writes in his book *The Prodigal Prophet*: 'Jesus did not merely weep for us; he died for us. Jonah went outside the city, hoping to witness its condemnation, but Jesus Christ went outside the city to die on a cross to accomplish its salvation.'[3]

Our complaints to God through lament are not only permissible, but encouraged because above all it is a relationship with us that God desires the most. Jonah wept bitterly to God because of God's mercy, but Jesus wept bitterly because he saw how his people wasted his Father's love.

Following the way of the Saviour who weeps is the only way we can find peace. We can lament and weep to our Saviour because he first wept and lamented to the Father. Jesus' tears showed a new way to face agony through the upside-down kingdom of God – it was only a weeping Saviour who triumphed over the grave.

Anger

Have you ever been so angry that you can barely speak? When you desperately want to get your point across, but find tears spilling from your eyes instead?

It happened a fair few times during the tumult of 2020, and as I first tried to write this chapter I was tempted to rant about a number of things. I wanted to rage against the injustices the coronavirus pandemic has exposed, the exacerbated suffering and lack of attention given to mental health issues; but on reflection, that's not the most helpful way to reflect on how we can lament in anger.

It has been said that anger is like fire; it can fuel you or kill you depending on how you use it and I'm a great believer in that. Anger can be the fuel which seeks to make change, in our own lives, in our churches and in our communities, but we have to be able to handle it with care.

In the wake of the Grenfell fire in 2017, worsened by unsafe cladding, social media called for two ways to respond: a day of prayer and a day of rage. Observing on Twitter, I saw lots of rage at the injustice and the tragedy, the undeniable evidence of a staggering gap between the rich and the poor. Over 500 people gathered to protest against the government's response to the Grenfell fire.

On the other hand, there were calls that Christians should be rejecting rage in favour of prayer, renaming the day as a day of prayer. As I watched, I wondered why they needed to be two separate days. Anger isn't a sin – it's a necessary force – and I don't think that rage and prayer are mutually exclusive. I can understand the fears that a march would be overrun with violence, but I don't think that rage needs to lead to violence.

The word 'rage' can be used to describe 'violent uncontrollable anger' but it can also mean 'a vehement desire or passion'. I expect the marchers had a bit of both because the fire that destroyed lives and homes need not have been so catastrophic.

Rage can be the catalyst for change, the start of something new. We have seen throughout history that people's anger can and does make a difference – we just have to be sure that our rage is directed into creative action, rather than destruction. We see this in Dylan Thomas' poem 'Do not go gentle into that good night' when he declares war on the coming of death, the night.

It seems to me that Jesus' anger in the temple forecourts looked a little bit like this. We aren't told if tears of frustration fell as he turned over tables, but we can begin to imagine the devastation and rage Jesus felt as he surveyed what was happening in his Father's house.

And when Jesus exclaimed, 'My house will be called a house of prayer for all the nations' as recounted in Mark 11.17, he was doing so in the presence of Gentiles. Many believed that the Messiah would purge the temple of Gentiles and yet here was Jesus welcoming them.

He wasn't just turning over the tables, he was turning over their way of thinking. All too often, we don't do well with anger and rage as Christians. We see them as 'bad' emotions and yet here is Jesus, angry at the misuse of his Father's house.

It is not anger and rage that are the sins – but for many, uncontrolled anger and rage fuel sin.

And yet Jesus did not sin.

Rage can be the catalyst for change, the start of something new. We have seen throughout history that people's anger can and does make a difference – we just have to be sure that our rage is directed into creative action, rather than destruction.

It was the injustice of what was happening in the temple that enraged Jesus – and he wanted to see change. I want to rage when I see schoolchildren going hungry in the holidays because their parents can't afford to feed them without their term-time free school meal provision. I want to rage when I see the effects of climate change on the poorest people in our world. I want to rage when I see people unable to access proper care and treatment for their mental health problems because of stigma and lack of funding.

Rage can propel us to fight for change when we let it be a power of creation rather than destruction.

Mark's Gospel tells us that after this episode in the temple people were 'amazed' by Jesus' teaching. His actions were not just those of thoughtless vandalism, they were a visual representation of his message – the gospel that welcomes sinners, that fuels change.

Our rage can be transformed by God when we bring it before him in lament. Walter Brueggemann writes: 'the laments are refusals to settle for the way things are. They are acts of relentless hope that believes no situation falls outside Yahweh's capacity for transformation. No situation falls outside of Yahweh's responsibility.'[4]

Jesus' anger was an act of hope-filled defiance to show Israelites and Gentiles that change was coming. We have to bring our anger to God in lament to allow him to empower our own hope-filled defiance to see change.

Fidelity

Betrayal elicits a particular type of pain; it's as bitter as the love shared was once sweet, isn't it? In the final week of his life, Jesus was betrayed over and again by the people closest to him, and yet he never abandoned them. Our laments may express feelings of abandonment, but the reality is that Jesus never betrays or abandons his people – even as he himself was betrayed and abandoned.

Judas' kiss – meant to be a sign of love – signed Jesus' death warrant. Perhaps he never truly knew the love of Jesus, but if he had once loved Jesus it was eclipsed by his other loves: money and power.

When Mark tells the story of the plot to kill Jesus and Judas' subsequent betrayal, he uses one of his most popular literary devices, known as the Markan sandwich, where he takes one story within his Gospel (in this case the plot to kill Jesus) and inserts it inside another story (the anointing of Jesus); this serves the purpose of giving both stories a greater sense of meaning. Here we see the betrayal and scheming of the Jewish leaders and Judas contrasted starkly with the story of the woman's devotion and fidelity.

The story of Jesus' anointing is one of worship and devotion. We read that Jesus is reclining at the table, a sign he was relaxed with the company he was keeping – among friends – but the woman who anoints Jesus remains unnamed. In fact, we hear more about the oil Jesus is anointed with than about the woman who anoints him; it's an expensive oil and the whole jar is broken over Jesus. While those surveying the event chastise the woman for her wastefulness, Jesus calls the woman's actions 'a beautiful thing'. The beauty of her devotion shines amid the ugliness of Judas' betrayal and yet Jesus makes it clear that her actions will anoint his body for burial – pointing forward to the agony that was in store for him.

Perhaps Judas wanted a warrior king instead of a servant king who wept and allowed himself to be anointed by unknown women. Whatever the truth he was willing to betray Jesus without ever truly understanding him, but the cost of his betrayal was too high and he took his own life.

The experience of betrayal not only destroys relationships – but also the trust that new relationships may be faithful – and it's why God's fidelity to us even when we are angry, grieving or complaining, is vital to our relationship with him.

It is a tragic end to the story – not just because Judas' life ended in suicide, but because he never really understood the gentleness and grace with which Jesus attracted people. Betrayal can beat people down, erode their confidence, faith and their view of God, but I hope that we can see that Jesus does not betray his people; he is faithful.

Judas' betrayal points us to Jesus' own faithfulness to the Father and to us.

He walked through Holy Week knowing what was coming, yet obeying his Father, loving his people faithfully to the cross and beyond.

Grief

The picture of Jesus in the garden of Gethsemane is one which never fails to bring a lump to my throat. It is the greatest agony ever experienced; and yet he did not run or swerve from the job ahead of him. It is the most profound grief ever experienced and it is done for our sake.

What makes it most captivating for me, though, is that even though Jesus knew the reason he was going to face the cross, it did not stop him lamenting to the Father in his distress. 'My Father, if it is possible, may this cup be taken from me. Yet not as I will, but as you will.'

It was not that Jesus was rejecting the path that lay ahead, but the weight of his grief and pain was such that he had to bring it to his Father. Jesus did not hold back in his expression of grief. Mark 14.34, 'My soul is overwhelmed with sorrow to the point of death', shows this is no ordinary grief, but the weight of the grief and pain of humanity that would be taken (and defeated) at the cross. Jesus' expression of grief shows, in the words of Mark Vroegop, that 'lament is how Christians grieve'.[5]

The picture of Jesus at Gethsemane is a reminder of the inescapable relationship between grief and love; one cannot exist without the other. Dr Colin Murray Parkes remarked:

The pain of grief is just as much part of life as the joy of love: it is perhaps the price we pay for love, the cost of commitment. To ignore this fact, or to pretend that it is not so, is to put on emotional blinkers which leave us unprepared for the losses that will inevitably occur in our own lives and unprepared to help others cope with losses in theirs.[6]

'Grief is the price we pay for love' was famously quoted by Queen Elizabeth II in a speech after the 9/11 terrorist attacks on the Twin Towers and Pentagon building back in 2001 and I think Gethsemane demonstrates this – it's the price of grief that Jesus paid for his love for us.

The events of Holy Week demonstrate Jesus' love for humanity in the most beautiful way and it is on Jesus' love that our laments rest. Jesus gave up his spirit. Then the darkness. The torn temple curtain. The world changed forever in a moment. For us.

Timothy Keller writes: 'Look at him facing the darkness for you. That'll enable you to face any darkness yourself.'[7]

It's a stunning truth which gives me great courage, because the darkness Jesus faced on the cross as he died cannot be imagined nor underestimated. It was a darkness which swallowed the midday sun; but it was a liberation which tore the temple curtain in two allowing entry to the holiest of holies. Whenever we feel as if no one understands our agony, we can remember the cross. Whenever we feel alone, our cries are joined with Jesus' as he echoed the psalmist's words of lament: 'My God, my God, why have your forsaken me?'

The cross is the beginning and end of our laments; the beginning because it ushers us into a new understanding of how far Jesus goes for us and the end because death's sting is extinguished.

As we know, the story doesn't end on Good Friday with the sky falling dark and neither does it skip forward to resurrection day. Scripture tells us very little about the day after Good Friday. It's often called 'Holy Saturday' and yet it is the day the Son of God himself was dead in the grave. It speaks to me that we cannot skip over the 'valley of the shadow of death', the pain of this life, our feelings of agony and abandonment, but instead asks the question of us: 'can we remain in the grief until it is through with us?'[8]

I wrote about it in my first book, *Learning to Breathe*, reflecting on the day God was in the grave:

It's the place where we spiritually live so often, when the worst has happened and we don't know if or how we can go on – yet in the midst of darkness we trust that dawn will break. It's often like this in the rest of life, I think. We often remember the most dramatic days, the happiest, but how often do we remember the days of silence, when everything is wrong but nothing can be done? I don't know if it's a good thing that we forget days like these in our own lives, but I think it would be good if we spent a little more time remembering Holy Saturday.[9]

Even now, some thirteen years after the light of my hope was snuffed out when I tried to take my own life, I live with the reality and each year, when the date rolls around again, I remember. I find I must grieve and lament the roads I travelled before I can fix my eyes once more on the author and perfecter of the faith that was so formed and transformed in my darkest nights of the soul. Recognizing and lamenting the despair of Holy Saturday has become foundational in the way I seek hope, both for my memories and in the life I lead now. It is a lesson in waiting in the dark for the dawn with lament – but it's not the end of the story – we don't end in lament because it enables us to look forward to hope.

Hope was not just born on Easter morning for me, but as Jesus committed his spirit into God's hands because it was then that he reached out to death so that we may live, then that he tasted hell so that we may taste heaven.

It's why we call the worst day in history 'good' and the day that follows 'holy'. It's the reason for our hope.

Questions for reflection

1 What are your experiences around repentance? Does it have positive or negative connotations?
2 Do you give things up for Lent? How might you incorporate lamenting into your prayer life over Lent instead of, or as well as, fasting from something?
3 When you are next faced with feelings of grief, anger, betrayal or complaint against God, find psalms which express those emotions and reflect on them using a journalling Bible.
4 How might you practise lament during Holy Week? For example, expressing anger at the injustice as Jesus did when he overturned the tables in the Temple court, holding a Holy Saturday vigil or a sunrise service.
5 Using Psalm 38 as a guide, offer a prayer of repentance and lament.

5

Easter: hoping

Hoping through tears

'Now Mary stood outside the tomb crying.' John's account of Jesus' first resurrection appearance begins with tears. The greatest day of all time, the root of our joy, begins with grief. The tears of Good Friday and Holy Saturday were still wet on the faces of Jesus' friends when he returned to them. They'd barely had a chance to process the agony of the worst day of their lives when their Saviour and friend had been killed, taking with him their hopes for the future, before everything changed all over again.

We don't know a great deal about Mary Magdalene, but we hear in Luke's Gospel that she has been freed from seven demons by Jesus. We don't know the nature of the demons, but biblically seven is often used to denote completion, so we can gather that she suffered a great deal before she was healed by Jesus. She's a woman who knew pain and rejection, but she was also present alongside Jesus in his final, darkest days, beside the cross and then as soon as the Sabbath was over she went to visit his tomb.

It was likely that Mary was going to clean and embalm Jesus' body ready for burial; through her grief, she seeks to serve the man who changed her life, in whom she found healing and freedom. In the first instance, to discover an empty tomb would have been a gut punch, she would have presumed that Jesus' body had been stolen and she would have been denied the process of caring for his body.

It's something people are all too aware of in the wake of the COVID-19 pandemic; as I wrote these words my grandma's life was drawing to a close in a care home miles away. When my grandpa died a few years ago, our whole family were able to visit regularly in his final weeks and days, to hold his hand and dry one another's tears as we first faced his death and then mourned the loss of him.

For my grandma, however, the picture was very different. My final meeting with her was behind a mask, wearing a surgical gown and plastic gloves. I was able to hold her hand and speak softly to her, but the arms of the woman who held me countless times over the years were empty in order to keep everyone safe.

In fact, I don't think I appreciated until this week the depth of distress the sight of the empty tomb would have caused Mary. Over the past year, thousands of people have been unable to say goodbye in the way they'd like to the people they loved and lost and have been left not only to mourn the person, but also the way in which they had to say goodbye.

And yet, in the midst of the agonizing shock and grief, comes the greatest surprise the world has ever seen.

John's Gospel, 20.11–18, records the tears that fell from Mary's eyes three times, and it strikes me that he's reaffirming how strange and unexpected it was that Jesus chose to present himself in the way he did.

In the early morning light, with her eyes blinded by tears and confused about where the body of the Saviour she loved had gone, perhaps it is no wonder that Mary does not recognize Jesus, and the fact that she mistakes him as the gardener contains its own beautiful truth. As Rachel Held Evans wrote: 'No wonder Mary Magdalene mistook the risen Jesus for a gardener. A new Tree of Life has broken through the soil and is stretching up toward the sun.'[1]

In fact, it isn't until Jesus speaks Mary's name that she finally realizes who she is seeing through her tears. Verse 16 recounts: 'Jesus said to her, "Mary." She turned toward him and cried out in Aramaic, "Rabboni" (which means "Teacher").'

It must have felt like a dream. Perhaps Mary wondered if she was dreaming, but she believed that she had seen her Saviour, alive and risen from the grave, and it was Mary who was entrusted with this most precious news.

It's worth noting that the testimony of a woman was not allowed in a Jewish court of law, the world in which Mary lived put no value on her words and yet it is Mary, a woman, who has suffered greatly and worshipped faithfully who is entrusted to share the news of Jesus' resurrection, perhaps with her eyes still brimming with tears.

The first sign of life we give as tiny babies is our cry; it's the sound that parents wait for, their own breath baited when a baby at last makes their entrance. So perhaps it is not so strange that Jesus appears first through tears. Our tears are our sign of life and they are a sign here of the new life Jesus offers, the new hope he embodies now that he has taken our sorrow to the grave and that one day every tear will be wiped away.

This is how the hope of God shows up time and again, both in Scripture and today. It shows up through our brokenness, through our tears, through our scars and reminds us that the kingdom of God is 'now and not yet'; it's arrived and yet we ache as we wait for its fulfilment. Even though Mary's reunion with the risen Lord is perhaps not how she might have imagined (if she ever had imagined something so audacious amid her grief), she proclaims 'I have seen the Lord' and tells her story. Matthew's Gospel tells us that Mary fled from the tomb 'with fear and great joy'; even here, joy, discomfort and fear sit together, just as they had when Mary, the mother of God, hears that the child she is bearing as a virgin is the Son of God. Fear and joy are the hallmarks of Jesus' life from beginning to end and beyond. As the priest Stephen Conway writes: 'We are called to the same joy; but we cannot ignore the fact that joy is always imperfect, fragile and threatened.'[2]

If it was surprising for early Christians to read that Jesus' first post-resurrection appearance was to a woman, perhaps it was even more so that he spent the morning hanging out with a couple of heartbroken friends on the road to Emmaus.

Walking with hope

Many of us spent much of 2020 going on walks, cramming conversations about life and death, love and loss into the allowed social interaction and there is something about the rhythm of walking that enables conversation (even though on a personal note I find coffee shops preferable to walks in the rain). There are things it's easier to say to the rhythm of a walk where both are looking ahead than when sitting face to face.

I expect that when Jesus joined Cleopas and his unnamed friend on their 'long-faced' walk through a haze of grief to Emmaus and began asking what was wrong with them, it was akin to an alien landing and asking us why we have such strong feelings about 2020.

It would have been the talk of the whole community: the story of that Friday, the freeing of Barabbas, the crucifixion of Jesus when they'd hoped he'd be the one to free them from Roman rule, the darkness, the torn temple curtain. And of course Jesus knew the story, it was his story, but the first part of the journey is about Jesus listening to Cleopas.

It's something that still strikes me as shocking. Jesus – who was there when the stars were placed into the night sky and the sea was separated from the land – listens to a heartbroken Cleopas. The heartbreak isn't unique to Cleopas and his friend; their words 'we had hoped he was the one' resound through the millennia to the hurting here and now.

What this passage in Luke 24 shows me more than anything, however, is summed up in the words of writer, Matt Bays, who says:

> Sometimes it feels as if God has invited himself into my pain, when I had hoped to be invited into his healing. We want a God who heals our wounds, but it seems we have a God who heals our hearts.[3]

When Jesus finally does speak, in our translations it can sound a little harsh, but theologian J. I. Packer writes, 'Jesus' tone is compassionate, not contemptuous; "O you dear silly souls" would get the nuance.' We don't see Jesus tell off Cleopas for his inability to see clearly; we see Jesus wanting to reveal something of his own story. Because that's what Jesus does next. He tells his story: verse 27 says, 'And beginning with Moses and all the Prophets, he explained to them what was said in all the Scriptures concerning himself.'

After listening to Cleopas' story, Jesus tells his own. He walks Cleopas through everything the Scriptures say about him. I can imagine Jesus taking Cleopas through Isaiah and the passages talking about the suffering servant, recounting the words of the psalm he cried on the cross 'My God, my God, why have you forsaken me?' It isn't always easy to tell our own stories, particularly the hard parts. It can be costly, but it can also reveal more of who is walking with us through our stories.

The first few of Jesus' appearances after his resurrection take place in ways that we can't comprehend, but which can't fail to bring comfort. They show us that the hope Jesus brings is for everyone and can show up in ways we might not ever expect.

He is seen through the tears of Mary and he walks alongside those whose hopes had been dashed. When Jesus walks alongside us in our dark nights of the soul, he reminds us of his story, heaven's hope and death's despair, and he lets us know that hope has the last word. And in times like the ones we are living through, with uncertain economies and rising mental illness, and daily news stories about the failure of services, it's a truth that we can hold on to tightly.

Frederick Buechner writes:

> I believe that whether we recognize him or not, or believe in him or not, or even know his name, again and again he comes and walks a little way with us along whatever road we're following. And I believe that through something that happens to us, or something we see, or somebody we know – who can ever guess how or when or where? – he offers us, the way he did at Emmaus, the bread of life, offers us new hope, a new vision of light that not even the dark world can overcome.[4]

Doubting and hoping

Jesus' resurrection appearances speak to the hardest emotions of human life: grief, hopelessness and, in the case of his meeting with apostle Thomas, doubt. I've always thought it's a bit harsh that Thomas is known as 'Doubting Thomas' two millennia after he expressed doubt in Jesus' resurrection; we don't call the apostle Peter 'Denying Peter', do we?! And as the story of Thomas' meeting with Jesus tells us, doubt is not the opposite or end of faith, but can be the beginning of a fresh and enlivened relationship with Jesus.

For some reason, Thomas was not with the other disciples the first time they encountered Jesus in the upper room and when they tell him 'We have seen the Lord!' he does not believe them. He replies, 'Unless I see the nail marks in his hand and put my finger where the nails were, and put my hand into his side, I will not believe.'

Some writers, such as John Calvin, have been quite scathing about Thomas' need for evidence of Jesus' resurrection. He writes, 'the stupidity of Thomas was astonishing and monstrous; for he was not satisfied with merely beholding Christ'.[5] But after all the disciples had seen and endured, the grief and confusion they would have felt at Jesus' death, I can't say that Thomas' reaction is far from what mine might have been.

In contrast, Dallas Willard points out:

> Let's remember that Jesus didn't leave Thomas to suffer without the blessing of faith and confidence; he gave him the evidence he required. That is typical of Jesus's approach to doubt; he responded to honest doubters in the way he knew best, the way that would help them to move from doubt to knowledge.[6]

There is a gentleness in the way Jesus responded to Thomas' doubt which gives me hope and is a reminder that doubt does not stand in defiance of faith, but as a complicated part of a relationship with Jesus. I've been a Christian since I was five years old and, as the years have passed, my questions and doubts have grown almost in tandem with my faith. They have been at the centre of my laments: as I've questioned where God is when life hurts, how he can stand to watch as his people hurt. But they've also been where I've experienced some of the greatest joy in my faith, not because I've been given answers, but because I've been broken open more to the character of God who deals with our laments and our doubts gently. It seems that God values our honesty and humanity, rather than our certainty. As Austin Fischer writes in his book *Faith in the Shadows*: 'Owning our uncertainty does not make our faith less credible, but more credible since it makes our faith more human and thus more honest.'[7]

John's focus in this passage is also on relationship rather than certainty: in writing, he seems not to highlight the doubt but rather Jesus' wounds, as when later in the passage he recounts Thomas' encounter with the risen Jesus, the focal point is that Jesus invites Thomas to touch his wounds. Earlier in the passage when Jesus first appears to the disciples in the locked room it is Jesus who shows the disciples his wounds.

Wounds that remain

Jesus is not unmarked by his ordeal, and it's a recognition of wounds that remain that trauma leaves a lasting legacy. Over the past 20 years, there has been a growing recognition that trauma is not limited to those who have been on the battle-fields of war; trauma is the response to any situation in which you feel under threat or powerless. For many, the COVID-19 pandemic has been a crash course in trauma; whether or not you were personally affected by the illness, the world seemed to stop overnight. Those on the front line of medicine and key workers faced danger more directly without the protection of being able to stay at home and limit as much social contact as possible in order to reduce the possibility of infection from coronavirus.

As the weeks and months rolled on, the trauma has been clear: whether it be from facing death on the wards, losing a loved one or the effect of lockdown on mental health, the cancellation of life-saving operations or the loss of face-to-face learning and socialization that children and young people have endured. What follows will be the whole world facing the aftermath of trauma, of tending to wounds even though the wounding is over. This is the story of Easter as much as the triumph over the grave; the vignettes of Mary Magdalene and Thomas demonstrate that there is life and hope amid the wounding and that it's found in the person of Jesus.

Diane Langberg writes in her book *Suffering and the Heart of God*: 'The message of the scars in the resurrected Christ is not that the resurrection takes the suffering away, but rather that the resurrection catches it up into God's glory.'[8] This is what Jesus' encounters with Thomas and Mary show us, not that the painful things are wiped away by the resurrection, but that Jesus has entered into our midst.

In the face of trauma, such as the pandemic and what the disciples had gone through during the events of Holy Week, language falls short. We are left without the ability to tell the story of that which has so injured us, and we need images and symbols in order to bridge the gap between our pain, our present reality and the grief, and the reality of the damage that trauma has left in its wake.

John's Gospel points us to the images of 'breath, spirit and wounds . . . [which] function to tell the truth'[9] in the absence of language which can adequately describe the reality of Christ's arrest, Peter's denial of him, the empty tomb and the resurrected body of a man whose crucifixion they had watched. These key images help us to piece together a narrative that makes sense of all that has happened and find the hope that is hidden in the wounds of Christ.

Trauma studies consistently show the importance of story-telling in integrating that which so ruptured our lives into our stories. Memory is a strange beast, but I've found it helpful to think of our minds as a library and, while most of our experiences are date-stamped and filed in order, traumatic memories are unable to be filed. They float around, timeless and uncontained, which is why flashbacks and nightmares of traumatic memories feel as if they are happening in the present. Meg Warner writes: 'Trauma collapses time, so that it seems to the person having flashbacks that the events being replayed are not stored safely in the past, but happening in the present.'[10]

In the aftermath of suicide attempts in my teens, I could never piece together the narrative of what had happened. It was too traumatic for my mind to understand and yet the absence of a proper memory tormented me; I wanted to remember the experience with a beginning and an end to put it in my past. I was frequently awoken with the sights and smells of the psychiatric ward, and the expressions of my loved ones burned behind my eyes filling me with shame. It wasn't until I gained access to my medical records, and was able to listen to the accounts of others who had walked with me through that time, that I began to write the story of what my family and I had been through and see how God had held us through it all. It was almost as if hearing the whole story, and then telling it myself by writing about it, enabled me to file it in my mind's library, remember it with sadness but not the all-consuming terror of flashbacks and nightmares.

In recent months I've often wondered if this is why wartime generations told and re-told their stories, in an attempt to come to terms with the horrors they experienced. I suspect that our generations will do the same as we recount the pandemic, the lockdowns and the social distancing that it required of us.

Communion

As we look through Scripture we see time and again the way in which stories are shared as a way of sharing history and coming to terms with the present. If John's Gospel uses breath, spirit and wounds, we can see how the accounts of the Last Supper and the re-enacting of it in Communion function in a similar way, facing the past so that we may look forward in both celebration and remembrance.

I used to really struggle with Communion. Years of struggling with self-harm meant that I found the talk of blood and bread incredibly painful – instead of realizing that I could come to the table with all my brokenness and baggage, I felt as though I had to arrive at the Communion table with everything 'sorted'. I didn't believe I was good enough to be there. I felt as though everything I had been through, everything I had done to myself, stood between me and Jesus.

The good news is that we don't have to wait to feel worthy to be worthy. We don't have to have faced our past to be accepted at God's table. Communion is not something to be ticked off a checklist – it's about accepting the invitation of grace that God offers us.

None of the men around the table with Jesus on Maundy Thursday could be considered worthy. In the three years they'd travelled with Jesus, they'd got into fights, battled for supremacy, missed the point more than once and, before the week was out, one would betray Jesus and another would deny him. And yet, despite their futures and their pasts, they can meet with Jesus – and the same is true for us. Communion is a way to understand our place in God's story using the most ordinary food – bread. Jesus blessed it, broke it and made it holy.

Glenn Packiam writes in his book *Blessed, Broken, Given*:

> Could it be that God's grace comes rushing into the
> very brokenness of our lives? Maybe brokenness has a
> way of opening us up to the Lord. The more aware we
> become of our frailty, the more we are able to embrace the
> grace of God. 'My strength is made perfect in weakness'
> the Lord told the apostle Paul (2 Corinthians 12.9). Or
> as Leonard Cohen sang, 'There is a crack, a crack in
> everything. That's how the light gets in.' To be broken is
> to be opened up to grace.[11]

The Communion bread tells the same story. The bread is
broken – but in its breaking it can be shared. The broken body
of Jesus allowed the grace and love of God to be shared with the
whole world. It tells us that however we begin, our past is never
the end of the story because God's grace is an interruption
which can make our lives more beautiful and more purposeful
than they ever could have been without the brokenness.

The reason for our hope does not end with Jesus' broken body
or even his resurrection and the marks of his wounds, but
with the promise of his everlasting presence and help.

With you

Matthew's Gospel alone records the words of the great com-
mission; the final words of his Gospel are, in my humble
opinion, some of the most beautiful: 'And surely I am with
you always, to the very end of the age' (Matthew 28.20). These

words are another of the bricks on which our assurance is built: that while Jesus' earthly ministry did not last for ever, it was the beginning of a new closeness between God and humanity which does last for ever. The Easter story is one of faith under pressure, of how our honesty with God through our doubts and lament are met with God's gentleness through Jesus who not only took our doubt and lament to the cross, but defeated them there and promises us a future filled with the presence of his Holy Spirit.

The same spirit which hovered over the surface of the earth in the creation narrative, that breathes new life into dry bones, descends on Jesus at his baptism and anoints the apostles at the beginning of their ministry after Jesus' ascension, still breathes on us today, sharing our groans and interceding on our behalf in our sorrows and enriching our joy in Jesus Christ. It brings peace which is the fullness of God's shalom, the wholeness and well-being that Adam and Eve lived with in Eden and it's what we have craved ever since we left the garden. Jesus is shalom in person and the Spirit is the gift of shalom for us all to experience until we are welcomed home.

Questions for reflection

1 How comfortable do you feel expressing different emotions in your place of worship? What might improve or change how you feel about expressing emotions in church?
2 What does it say about Jesus that he chose to reveal himself to women, whose testimony wasn't trusted in courts? How might that impact how we lead with or as women?

3 Take a walk either on your own or with a friend, reflect on the words 'we had hoped' and offer your own prayers of hope and hopelessness to God.

4 How do you feel when you experience doubts about your faith? Does Jesus' encounter with Thomas encourage or challenge you?

5 Next time you take Communion, reflect on the story of the Last Supper and invite God to fill the places of your brokenness with his grace. Perhaps consider holding your own Passover supper with family and friends before Easter to help connect with the narrative of Holy Week.

6 Trace the events of Holy Week through Psalm 102.

6

Ordinary Time: rejoicing

When I first started to think about writing this book, I asked on Twitter and Instagram for the best books on joy from a Christian perspective. Almost all the answers included some kind of reference to Paul's letter to the Philippians in the Bible. It's sometimes known as the epistle of joy in which Paul tells the Philippians how to live with joy in an often less than joyful world. In short, it teaches us to rejoice, to seek and find joy in every season of life.

All too often, Paul's words are used as sticking plasters for wounds of anxiety, and yet Philippians is a letter written to a church of retired Roman soldiers who supported Paul when they heard about his imprisonment. It's a letter full of warmth and hope, beginning with words of fondness. Verses 3 and 4 make this clear: 'I thank my God every time I remember you. In all my prayers for all of you, I always pray with joy'; the whole book is one encouraging prayerfulness and joy amid affliction. Miroslav Volf calls it 'an expression of joy and an invitation to joy',[1] indeed, the word joy appears some 16 times in this short letter!

Upside down joy

Paul's letter to the Philippians turns our idea of joy upside down for there is little earthly reason for Paul to be happy. He has been imprisoned for disturbing the city and Roman jails were anything but comfortable, so the fact that he speaks of joy from prison makes it plain that Paul isn't offering twee encouragement, but rather a testimony of finding the source of joy and contentment even in the hardest and unhappiest of times. Biblical commentator Fred Craddock writes, 'Paul knows that if [the Philippians] can see that he remains joyful, they might recover their own.'[2]

Paul's invitation to joy for the Philippians is threefold: encouraging them in thanksgiving, humility and steadfastness.

Thanksgiving

In recent years, there has been a wealth of research gathered supporting the value of gratitude and thanksgiving. Paul's letter to the Philippians is, ostensibly, a thank you letter for their support. I remember when I was younger that after every Christmas and birthday, I'd get to choose some notes or cards to send to those people who had sent me presents; today it's more likely to be a text, but there is something about a handwritten note which conveys thanks in a more significant way. Gratitude is the expression of appreciation for what someone has[3] and can be both a mood and a personality trait; we can feel grateful, but we can also make the decision to be grateful through practices such as gratitude journals or using the popular hashtag #threegoodthings on social media.

Studies have consistently shown countless benefits for physical, social, spiritual and emotional health – from providing protection from stress and depression, increased life satisfaction,[4] lower reporting of aches and pains, to increased empathy, better sleep and higher levels of resilience.[5] Gratitude in and of itself can increase our joy, but I don't think that's why Paul expresses thanksgiving so readily in his letters: his interest lies not in the positive psychological benefits, but in putting his present situation in an eternal perspective – and encouraging others to do the same.

In a similar vein, he writes in his letter to the Roman church: 'I consider that our present sufferings are not worth comparing with the glory that will be revealed in us. For the creation waits in eager expectation for the children of God to be revealed' (Romans 8.18–19). At first glance, it can feel like a get-out clause for the problem of pain and faith, that what we go through on earth is irrelevant compared to the glories of heaven; but Paul writes as one acquainted with pain. Paul is not talking from a life without trouble. Most of the letters we have included in our Bible written by Paul are written from a prison cell. I don't think he is diminishing the suffering we share in life: he's saying that the suffering, although great, is nothing compared to what is to come. He's also not saying that suffering is a prerequisite to glory. What he is setting out is a vision for something so beautiful and so indescribable that our pain can't compare – hope. Hope is the reason for our thanksgiving, because Jesus is hope incarnate.

Humility

Jesus isn't just hope incarnate; he's humility incarnate. The famous words of the hymn contained in Philippians 2 explore Paul's reason for joy in the gospel by retelling the story of Jesus' life, death and resurrection and looking forward to

Christ's return. As we've seen throughout our journey looking at joy and lament, it is Jesus who is the reason for our joy and the reason we can bring both our joys and our laments to God.

Jesus is the embodiment of humility; he didn't think less of himself but rather was secure in his identity as God's child and so felt no need to have others think well of him. So often, I think we misunderstand humility; we think that it means downplaying ourselves and our abilities rather than viewing ourselves rightly. But joy isn't found in thinking badly of ourselves and neither is it found in puffing ourselves up!

We live in an age of the #humblebrag where a boast is disguised as humility or a complaint and our social media feeds are full of them: from the celebrity tweeting about choosing multiple outfits for all their award ceremonies, to people who display their charitable endeavours for all to see with a self-deprecating caption. This is the opposite of humility, which Rick Warren so eloquently described as 'not thinking less of yourself, it's thinking of yourself less'.[6] It's how Jesus lived his life and how he preached, shunning those things that would have elevated him from the manger, the donkey and the cross.

Humility leads us to rejoicing in what God does through and for us because we are reminded who we are – and whose we are. It reminds us to rely on the steadfastness of God, not our own strength.

Steadfastness

Paul reminds the Philippians throughout his letter that the reason for his joy, and the reason they can inhabit joy, is because of Jesus' steadfast love – joy starts with Jesus' love. The word steadfastness can be likened to the Hebrew word 'hesed' which is translated as 'loving kindness' as we saw when we looked at the book of Lamentations. In the Old Testament, the people of God rejoiced because of what God had done for them, whereas in the New Testament we rejoice in the person and work of Jesus Christ.

The command to 'rejoice in the Lord', therefore, is one that reminds us that our joy can only be found in God. It's not happy circumstances but the steadfast loving kindness of God which is shown most beautifully in the person and work of Jesus who was born, died, rose again and sent the Holy Spirit to give his people peace. Philippians 4.4–6 proclaims:

> Rejoice in the Lord always. I will say it again: rejoice! Let your gentleness be evident to all. The Lord is near. Do not be anxious about anything, but in every situation, by prayer and petition, with thanksgiving, present your requests to God. And the peace of God, which transcends all understanding, will guard your hearts and minds in Christ Jesus.

Anxiety

All too often, this particular passage has been used as a way to guilt people of faith into believing that their struggles with anxiety and mental health are some kind of failure of faith, as if having an anxiety disorder is somehow a result of personal sin.

And yet, if we trace the Bible's teaching on anxiety from its first mention in Genesis, we see an altogether different picture.

Genesis 3.10 records that upon discovering their nakedness and attempting to hide from God, Adam says: 'I heard you in the garden, and I was afraid because I was naked; so I hid.' It wasn't until after sin entered the world at the Fall that fear and anxiety were also mentioned for the first time.

Anxiety, in and of itself, is not a bad thing; it is designed to keep us safe and responding appropriately to threats to our life by allowing us to fight the threat ahead of us, freeze (which historically meant being able to play dead in the face of a physical threat to our lives) or fly (get as far away as possible from the threat). These reactions were particularly useful when the threats were all physical (like a lion approaching) but are less helpful when the threats faced are things like exams or driving tests.

It's also important here to make a distinction between anxiety and worry. Anxiety is the physiological response to a threat and is not something we can directly control, whereas worry is more rumination. For example, when Jesus speaks of worry in the Sermon on the Mount, he uses examples such as worrying about food and clothing, whereas anxiety relates more directly to threats to life. I believe it is possible to 'worry less' – but we always need anxiety as it keeps us safe – even though it doesn't feel good.

When it comes to the anxiety faced by Adam and Eve because of their nakedness, God's response is gracious, despite the fact that it's the result of their own sin. God does not stop them experiencing the consequences of their sin, but he does clothe them out of compassion for them.

Similarly, when commands against fear or anxiety are made throughout the Bible, they are always backed up with reminders of the character of God and the reason that people may be comforted in their anxiety. In the verses in Philippians, we are encouraged not to be anxious – not because it's sinful or a flaw in our characters – but because we can access the all-encompassing peace of God through prayer. The J. B. Phillips translation puts it like this:

> Don't worry over anything whatever; tell God every detail of your needs in earnest and thankful prayer, and the peace of God which transcends human understanding, will keep constant guard over your hearts and minds as they rest in Christ Jesus.

It's not a call to shame, but a reminder that all our fear and pain can be brought to Christ.

Perhaps the most beautiful example of this is Jesus' experience of anxiety on the Mount of Olives the night before he was crucified, as recounted in Luke 22. When he prays the night before his crucifixion, Luke's Gospel recounts that Jesus' sweat fell like drops of blood to the ground (Luke 22.44). This is actually an incredibly rare condition called hematidrosis where extreme anxiety causes capillary glands to burst, meaning our sweat has blood in it. Anxiety of this severity is one few could endure and yet Jesus experiences it for our sake. Jesus is not reprimanded or sinning when he feels this anxiety, but he does provide a pattern for us to take our most difficult feelings to God in prayer, to wrestle with him.

Wrestling for blessing

To wrestle with God is part of lament and it's part of the path to joy. In the Old Testament we hear about the blessings of God bestowed on those who follow him, from his promises to Abraham to the stolen blessing in the story of Jacob.

Perhaps the strangest account of blessing occurs in the life of Jacob, who first steals the blessing meant for his older brother Esau and then receives a blessing from God after wrestling with him – indeed Jacob's name means 'he grasps the heel', a Hebrew idiom for 'he deceives'. He received the birthright blessing through deception – and his name does not allow him to forget it.

Isaac conveys a blessing on Jacob meant for the firstborn of the family. Genesis 27.28–29 records that it spans from a blessing of 'heaven's dew and earth's richness – an abundance of grain and new wine' to the responsibility to 'be lord over your brothers', as well as the promise that 'those who curse you be cursed and may those who bless you be blessed'.

The blessing unsurprisingly created enmity between the brothers and, as the narrative unfolds, we see Jacob receiving the blessings of land and family. But the blessing is also one of conflict and Jacob wrestled with God for his blessing (Genesis 32) right before a restoration of sorts between the two brothers.

Jacob's wrestle with God is not his first encounter with God in the dark, however; just a few chapters earlier we read of his encounter with angels as he fled for his life as the result of yet another conflict. Jacob's wrestle for blessing stands in contrast with how he stole his brother's birthright; for then it was a blessing he earned only through deceit and here it is a blessing through struggle.

Isn't it often the case for us that the blessings we receive through the struggles are all the more powerful? It seems that God works through our struggles to bless us as a reminder that blessings are not rights, or something that can be achieved through merit, but through the graciousness of God.

Jacob leaves this night-time encounter irrevocably changed: in name, in blessing and in his woundedness. It seems to me that Jacob's wrestling for blessing is lament in action, with its wonder and wounds.

We aren't told the identity of Jacob's adversary in this passage, but we are told of Jacob's new identity. No longer will he be known by his worst trait, but by the struggle he has survived; we see it time and again through the Bible, that name changes go to the heart of the new identities God bestows upon those who meet with him. From Abram who becomes Abraham, Jacob to Israel, Simon to Peter and Saul to Paul, there is no name change without an attendant struggle. The new names God bestows are ones which look forward in hope to the future with his blessing.

The new names are not a promise of life without struggle, though they are a promise of God's presence through struggle. Jacob leaves the encounter newly named – but also newly wounded – with a limp to show his struggle. Generations later Paul recounted that despite his new name he was not immune to being wounded but would carry his wounds as a testimony to the weakness in which he rejoiced.

In his second letter to the Corinthians, he writes:

> Three times I pleaded with the Lord to take it away from me. But he said to me, 'My grace is sufficient for you, for my power is made perfect in weakness.' Therefore I will boast all the more gladly about my weaknesses, so that Christ's power may rest on me. That is why, for Christ's sake, I delight in weaknesses, in insults, in hardships, in persecutions, in difficulties. For when I am weak, then I am strong.
> (2 Corinthians 12.8–10)

I cannot help but see parallels between Jacob and Paul: the encounters with God which changed everything for them – from Jacob's dreams and wrestles to Paul's blindness and wounding. The stories of both men demonstrate that the testimony of God's faithfulness can be shown to others through our woundedness.

We are often ashamed or protective over our wounded places and our scars, and yet they are often signs of what we have survived through God's grace. I spent many years barely able to survey the scars of my self-harm; they were the marks of my disgrace and inescapable reminders of the years of my life which most wounded my mind and my body.

And yet, scars by their very existence are testimony to a chapter of a story which has been survived. For me, scars are a reminder of how dark life became, but also of the grace of God which sustains me. I would probably still choose not to be marked with reminders but, as I am reminded of what hurt, I am also reminded of all that has been healed in the intervening years and of the sufficiency of God's grace and the constant need for me to rest my weakness in God's strength. Despite it all, they are marks of healing as much as wounding, of blessing as much as pain.

Jars of clay

In another of his letters, Paul writes about Christians having treasure in jars of clay. 2 Corinthians 4.7–9 says:

But we have this treasure in jars of clay to show that this all-surpassing power is from God and not from us. We are hard pressed on every side, but not crushed; perplexed, but not in despair; persecuted, but not abandoned; struck down, but not destroyed.

In the past I'd always assumed this treasure would have been completely hidden by the clay; I thought it meant that we had treasure hidden beneath ugliness, but I recently read that the jars of clay Paul was talking about were 'weaker' so that they could let the light through. When we are at our weakest, God shows his strength again and again. It might not change our immediate reality, but it can give us something to put our hope and our faith in; blessings enable us to share hope for those around us, too.

Blessings, both then and now, are steps on the road between brokenness and lament to joy. Blessing and lament do not seek to erase the brokenness, but to be markers of hope on the road before us.

Perhaps the most precious thing about blessings is that they are made to be shared. They are not to be hoarded and boasted about – but shared and rejoiced in – recognizing where they came from and how the blessing extends.

In the Old Testament, blessings were conferred through families, passed from father to eldest son, such as between Isaac and his sons, but Jesus made our definition of family wider and deeper. It's no longer limited by bloodline or national identity, but by anyone who has put their faith in Jesus.

Writer and poet Jan Richardson writes that:

> Blessings invoke God's care for all manner of people, activities and objects, illuminating the presence of the sacred that inhabits and intertwines with the ordinary . . . [they] convey God's desire for our wholeness and that [blessing] holds the ability to open us to the presence of God in any circumstance.[7]

Where lament speaks to the void where shalom should be, a blessing invokes God to send his shalom on those who trust in him and encourages those still longing for shalom that God has not abandoned his people and that joy can be found when we call out to him, whether in praise or petition. Perhaps we can say that blessings and laments are the two sides of the road to joy: one raging at what hurts and the other hoping for healing. When we leave our laments with God, we can share our blessings with one another.

I found myself doing just that at the beginning of the first lockdown in March 2020. I was screaming my laments to God, expressing my anger, fear and grief, while also composing blessings to share with the community on Instagram as a response to what I felt God was saying to my less than articulate laments. I've come to see that blessings are how we can share our joys and our laments communally; author of *Benedictus,* John O'Donohue, describes it like this: 'The language of blessing is invocation: a calling forth.'[8] So in the same way that warmer air invokes the buds of blossom to bloom, may our blessings to one another invoke the loving kindness of God among ourselves.

Rejoicing

Rejoicing is like the watermark of Paul's letter to the Philippians. It's a reminder to us to keep rejoicing in God when prayers are answered the way we'd like them to be, such as when Nehemiah rebuilt the walls of Jerusalem; when we are tasked with the unexpected like Mary; even (perhaps especially) when life is at its toughest, such as it was for the disciples as they grieved the death of their Saviour; and for the early church which strived to follow God amid political turmoil and persecution.

Further on in Philippians 4, Paul reminds the Philippians of another reason they can rejoice – because they and we are accompanied by the Spirit of God. Jesus did not leave his disciples alone to face the world without him, but sent the gift of the Holy Spirit who had once hovered over the surface of the deep before creation, who breathed life into the dry bones of Ezekiel's prophecy and falls on the apostles at Pentecost in power.

Philippians 4.12–13 encourages: 'I know what it is to be in need, and I know what it is to have plenty. I have learned the secret of being content in any and every situation, whether well fed or hungry, whether living in plenty or in want. I can do all this through him who gives me strength.' It almost seems to flow straight from Jesus' teaching on worry when he speaks about not worrying about the food you will eat or the clothes to wear. God clothed Adam and Eve in Eden when they felt their nakedness and Paul reminds us that contentment is not found in a full fridge (not that they had fridges but you get the picture!) but in seeking Jesus, resting in who he is and what he has done for us on the cross. In the words of Jennie Pollock, 'the secret is him'.[9] Jesus is the secret of contentment and joy because he gives us strength to face both our joys and sorrows and therefore the reason we can rejoice at all times.

The command you'll see in Philippians 4.4–7, is not to be happy at all times, that's not realistic, but to rest in the peace that is given by the Spirit.

Joy is included in the book of Galatians as one of the fruits of the Spirit, alongside love, peace, forbearance, goodness, faithfulness, gentleness and self-control (Galatians 5.22–23). These fruits are signs of life being lived in accordance with the Spirit – and joy is among them. It is a quality to practise as much as it is a gift.

Practising joy

So how do we practise joy?

To learn the language of lament, we looked back to the Scriptures and we need to do the same to practise joy.

We see joy bursting through music in the Psalms: Psalm 100 encourages us to 'Shout for joy to the Lord, all the earth. Worship the Lord with gladness; come before him with joyful songs.' There is joy in sharing, listening and joining in with music to praise God; it's one of the things we have missed most about corporate church life since the start of the pandemic. For months of the year music has only been heard in homes; more recently worship bands have played to empty churches to be live-streamed to living rooms, and Christian festivals like New Wine and Spring Harvest have been experienced through screens instead of physically joining together to sing praises. Perhaps it's this loss that has reaffirmed its importance; after rightly needing to encourage people that worship is more than sung praises, may we once again be able to cherish communal praise once restrictions allow.

We also practise joy through food and feasting. This is seen in the celebrations of Christmas around the dinner table, Communion that we share together, feasts borrowed and shared with our Jewish neighbours – such as Purim and Sabbath dinners. Food is inextricably linked with the joy of celebration.

Joy is also found in prayer, through connecting with our Creator, whether publicly or personally, out loud or in our hearts. We are given the gift of the Spirit who intercedes on our own behalf as Romans 8.26 promises. 'In the same way, the Spirit helps us in our weakness. We do not know what we ought to pray for, but the Spirit himself intercedes for us through wordless groans.' Our prayers do not need to be eloquent, they don't have to be micro sermons – they are the whispers of the heart and enable us to be in communion with God, whether or not our prayers are answered in the way we'd like them to be. Pete Greig, founder of the 24/7 prayer movement, writes in his book, *Dirty Glory*; 'A house of prayer is, according to Isaiah's original prophecy, meant to be marked out by joy.'[10] So often I think our view of prayer is that it must be sombre and controlled, but the Bible paints a picture of prayer which weeps, but also prayer which celebrates and rejoices as seen in Nehemiah and the Psalms.

Scripture speaks a lot about joy and it is most commonly found nestled with sorrow, particularly in the life of Jesus. Our joy is planted deep in the sorrow of Christ – our sorrow births our joys. Sorrow and joy cannot be separated because we cannot have one without the other when we make our home in the heart of God.

As writer Frederick Buechner so beautifully puts it:

Joy is home, and I believe the tears that came to our eyes were more than anything else, homesick tears. God created us in joy and created us for joy and in the long run not all the darkness there is in the world and in our selves can separate us finally from that joy, because whatever else it means to say God created us in his image . . . we have God's joy in our blood.[11]

I love this image of joy as coming home that Buechner gives, an image that we see throughout the Bible: from Adam and Eve leaving their home in Eden and the Israelites finding their home in the promised land, to Jesus' story of the prodigal son being welcomed home by his father and the Holy Spirit sent to give us a taste of our heavenly home. The path to joy is paved with lament; it's not easy and sometimes it will feel as though joy is too far away, but it is our journey home to our Creator and Redeemer.

And in the same way that once COVID restrictions are lifted, we will again embrace one another in our homes, so Jesus will one day call us home into his embrace. As he says in chapter 14 of John's Gospel:

'Do not let your hearts be troubled. You believe in God; believe also in me. My Father's house has many rooms; if that were not so, would I have told you that I am going there to prepare a place for you? And if I go and prepare a place for you, I will come back and take you to be with me that you also may be where I am. You know the way to the place where I am going . . . I am the way and the truth and the life. No one comes to the Father except through me. If you really know me, you will know my Father as well. From now on, you do know him and have seen him.'

Jesus' life, death, resurrection and ascension marks the pattern for our own journeys home to the Father's love, from which we were created – Jesus' journey home is one of joy paved with lament – and it is our journey, too.

Questions for reflection

1 Thanksgiving and gratitude have proven positive benefits. How might you incorporate practices of thanksgiving
into your devotional life?

2 We see throughout Scripture how important naming
is. Do you think names still have the same importance
today?

3 It's often been cited that we are living in an anxiety epidemic. What do you think contributes to the atmosphere
of anxiety and how can we encourage people living with
anxiety disorders?

4 Take some time to write your own blessing for whichever
season you're living through.

5 Meditate on the words of Psalm 103 and reflect on how
the character of God is presented in response to each
emotion conveyed.

Afterword

When I began to dream of this book; the idea of a national lockdown was only just beginning to edge into my mind. There was talk of social distancing and an unease in the air, but none of us could have imagined how the world would change or that in February 2021, as I write these words, we would be in lockdown three. The death toll is still too high, there are families and friends who have spent almost a year without holding each other, babies who have never known our 'old normal' and vulnerable men and women who have barely left their homes in a year.

And yet.

The first snowdrops have begun to appear, the cases have started to fall, there are whispers about an easing out of lockdown and millions are being vaccinated every week.

After a year of seemingly unending despair, hope is beginning to find its voice again.

It has been a year of extremes, the sharpest and most painful losses, but also a reconnection with lost and perhaps simpler joys. Our worlds have grown smaller, but that has made it easier to appreciate those in our world. A year ago I was dreaming of a hot beach somewhere on an all-inclusive holiday, the kind not particularly possible when accompanied by a toddler. Now I can say, hand on heart, that what I want more than cocktails by the beach is a playdate at home with my friends and our children. The coffee will probably grow cold, there might be a toddler tantrum and perhaps there will be some kind of spillage, but it will be full of the sweetest joy, as it is one of the things I've missed the most during this strangest of times.

I've also found a new appreciation for nature and creation. I have been an 'indoor' person for my whole life, far more content with the comforts of a hot drink and a good book than braving the elements. This year, however, as the world stopped, I began to notice the wonder that is all around us. From the first snowdrops of winter, the wild flowers of summer to the falling leaves of autumn, the message of light and life breaking through is all around us. Nature has taught me that joy can be found in the most unexpected places because God's fingerprints cover everything he has created. For example (and forgive me if this is a well-known fact for most!), I was astonished this year to discover that even as the leaves reveal their true colours in the autumn and begin to fall from the trees, substances are released by the tree to protect itself, as scar tissue does for us, and the crop for the next year is ready and waiting to bloom in the spring. God has designed the world in a way that illustrates 'yet'; the green leaves lose their colour, but reveal one true colour that's been there all along.

The natural world seems to re-enact resurrections over and again as death and life cycle over and again with the decay of fallen leaves providing the perfect conditions for new life to flourish.

But perhaps what I have learned most about this year is wonder. I've learnt it by watching the wonder this broken world provokes in my little boy. The wonder of birds huddled together, who scatter when he reaches them. The wonder of the flavour bursting in his mouth at his first taste of chocolate. The wonder of the twinkling fairy lights adorning the Christmas tree. His wonder has awakened my own, which has been dulled by the everyday. And even though the world is broken, even though life sometimes hurts – wonder remains God's fingerprint on creation. G. K. Chesterton wrote: 'We are perishing for want of wonder, not for want of wonders.' It's a reminder to pay attention to the hope that rises, even in the hardest of times.

And, as we have seen throughout this book, the pandemic isn't the only period that puts our passions and priorities into perspective. Throughout history – both our own and that of Christians throughout the ages – there has been the ebb and flow of joy and sorrow, waters rough and smooth. Throughout life our sense of 'normal' changes and we find ourselves fully immersed in a life that looks different to how we might have imagined it.

Similarly, there will be many more moments to come where we find ourselves acutely aware that the ground beneath us is shifting and our certainties are shaking. I believe that God is calling us to weep with those who weep when it feels like the rest of the world is rejoicing and sing with hope in our hearts in the face of suffering. Against all the odds God invites us to hold joy and lament in tension because he's big enough to hold all our humanity at once. And somehow, through these tensions, we can catch a glimpse afresh of our unchanging God in the ever-shifting sands of our world. I wonder what those moments are for you? What memories or hopes or fears for the future can you invite God's inexplicable grace and unfathomable peace into today?

Yet is the language of hoping against hope. It is believing that the new life of spring is hiding amongst what seems dead. It is the Creator of the world coming to save his world through a baby. It is that same Creator sending his beloved Son to die so that we may live.

It's my prayer that as, over the years to come, we begin to grieve the pandemic and other turning points in our stories of loss, change and new direction, we will bring these feelings and situations to God in lament, using Scripture as our guide and prayer as our compass to point us back north to our Creator.

Notes

1 Advent: waiting

1 C. Seitz, *Interpretation: Isaiah 1-39, a Bible commentary for teaching and preaching* (Louisville: John Knox Press, 2012), p. 87.

2 C. McNiel, *All Shall Be Well: Awakening to God's presence in his messy, abundant world* (Colorado Springs: NavPress, 2019), p. xxii.

3 B. Brown Taylor, *Learning to Walk in the Dark* (Norwich: Canterbury Press, 2014), p. 129.

4 P. Gooder, *The Meaning in the Waiting: The spirit of Advent* (Norwich: Canterbury Press, 2008), p. 147.

5 T. Keller, *Hidden Christmas: The surprising truth behind the birth of Christ* (London: Hodder and Stoughton, 2017), p. 119.

6 M. Guite, *Waiting on the Word* (Norwich: Canterbury Press, 2015).

7 S. Bessey, *Miracles and Other Reasonable Things: A story of unlearning and relearning God* (London: DLT, 2019), p. 54.

2 Christmas: celebrating

1 K. Bowler, *Everything Happens for a Reason: And other lies I've loved* (London: SPCK, 2018), p. xiii.

2 W. G. Morris, 'Joy', in S. B. Ferguson and D. Wright (eds), *Dictionary of Theology* (Leicester: IVP, 2005), p. 335.

3 F. Craddock, *Interpretation: Luke: A Bible commentary for teaching and preaching* (Louisville: John Knox Press), p. 40.

4 T. Keller, *Hidden Christmas: The surprising truth behind the birth of Christ* (London: Hodder and Stoughton, 2017), p. 117.

5 R. Held Evans, *Searching for Sunday: Loving, leaving and finding the Church* (Tennessee: Thomas Nelson, 2015), p. 208.

6 A. Heschel, *The Wisdom of Heschel* (New York: Farrar, Straus and Giroux, 1986).

7 H. Nouwen, *Following Jesus: Finding our way home in an age of anxiety* (London: SPCK, 2019), p. 130.

3 Ordinary Time: grieving

1 P. Scazzero, *Emotionally Healthy Spirituality* (Grand Rapids: Zondervan, 2017), p. 117.

2 T. Keller, *Walking with God through Pain and Suffering* (London: Hodder and Stoughton, 2015), p. 253.

3 P. Scazzero, *Emotionally Healthy Spirituality,* p. 123.

4 M. Yaconelli, *The Gift of Hard Things: Finding grace in unexpected places* (Downers Grove, Intervarsity Press, 2016), p. 102.

5 M. Duggan, *God Among the Ruins: Trust and transformation in difficult times* (Abingdon: The Bible Reading Fellowship, 2018), p. 869 (eBook).

6 N. Wolterstorff, *Lament for a Son* (Grand Rapids: William B. Eerdmans, 1987), p. 126.

7 I. Opie, ed., *The Oxford Dictionary of Nursery Rhymes* (Oxford: Oxford University Press, 1997), p. 254.

8 B. Slevcove, *Broken Hallelujahs: Learning to grieve the big and small losses of life* (Downers Grove: Intervarsity Press, 2016), p. 20.

9 'Footprints', <https://onlythebible.com/Poems/Footprints-in-the-Sand-Poem.html> (accessed 22/02/2021).

4 Lent: lamenting

1 J. Todd Billings, *Rejoicing in Lament: Wrestling with incurable cancer and life in Christ* (Grand Rapids: Brazos Press, 2016), p. 48.

2 M. Card, *Inexpressible: Hesed and the mystery of God's lovingkindness* (Downers Grove: Intervarsity Press, 2019), p. 3.

3 T. Keller, *The Prodigal Prophet: Jonah and the mystery of God's mercy* (London: Hodder and Stoughton, 2018), p. 124.

4 W. Brueggemann, 'A Shape for Old Testament Theology, II: Embrace of Pain', *The Catholic Biblical Quarterly*, vol. 47, no. 3 (July 1985), pp. 395–415 (available online at: <www.jstor.org/stable/43716986>, accessed 24/2/2021).

5 M. Vroegop, 'Lament leads to praise', <http://markvroegop.com/lament-leads-to-praise> (accessed 24/2/2021).

6 Dr Colin Murray Parkes, 'Inspirational quote 9.24.15 Grief is the price', <https://blog.aftertalk.com/inspirational-quote-9-24-15-grief-is-the-price> (accessed 6.1.21).

7 T. Keller, *Hidden Christmas: The surprising truth behind the birth of Christ* (London: Hodder and Stoughton, 2017), p. 69.

8 A. and C. Bauman, *A Brave Lament: For those who know death* (self-published, 2018), p. 22.

9 R. Newham, *Learning to Breathe: My journey with mental illness* (London: SPCK, 2018), p. 91.

5 Easter: hoping

1 R. Held Evans, *Searching for Sunday: Loving, leaving and finding the Church* (Tennessee: Thomas Nelson, 2015), p. 46.

2 S. Conway, 'A Good Easter' in M. Oakley (ed.), *A Good Year* (London: SPCK, 2016), p. 97.

3 M. Bays, *Finding God in the Ruins: How God redeems pain* (Eastbourne: David C. Cook, 2016), p. 133.

4 F. Buechner, *Secrets in the Dark: A life in sermons* (London: Harper Collins 2006), p. 257.

5 Quoted by S. Rambo in *Resurrecting Wounds: Living in the afterlife of trauma* (Waco: Baylor Press, 2017), p. 22.

6 D. Willard in *The Allure of Gentleness: Defending the faith in the manner of Jesus* (available online at: <https://www.goodreads.com/work/quotes/41700119-the-allure-of-gentleness-defending-the-faith-in-the-manner-of-jesus> (accessed 24/2/2021).

7 A. Fischer, *Faith in the Shadows: Finding Christ in the midst of doubt* (Downers Grove: Intervarsity Press, 2018), p. 20.

8 D. Langburg, *Suffering and the Heart of God: How trauma destroys and Christ restores* (Greensboro: New Growth Press, 2015).

9 S. Rambo, *Resurrecting Wounds*, p. 82.

10 M. Warner, *Joseph: a story of resilience* (London: SPCK, 2020), p. 11.

11 G. Packiam, *Blessed, Broken, Given: How your story becomes sacred in the hands of Jesus* (New York: Crown Publishing, 2019), p. 42.

6 Ordinary Time: rejoicing

1 M. Volf and J. Crisp (eds), *Joy and Human Flourishing: Essays on theology culture and the good life* (Minneapolis: Fortress Press, 2015).

2 F. Craddock, *Interpretation Commentary: Philippians: A Bible commentary for teaching and preaching* (Louisville: Westminster John Knox Press, 2011), p. 17.

3 'Gratitude', available online at <https://psychologytoday.com/intl/basics/gratitude> (accessed 17/02/2021).

4 M. Sarner, 'Is gratitude the secret of happiness? I spent a month finding out', *The Guardian*, 23 October 2018 (available online at <https://theguardian.com/lifeandstyle/2018/oct/23/is-gratitude-secret-of-happiness-i-spent-month-finding-out> (accessed 17/02/2021).

5 A. Morin, '7 Scientifically Proven Benefits Of Gratitude That Will Motivate You To Give Thanks Year-Round', Forbes, 23 November 2014 (available online at: <https://www.forbes.com/sites/amymorin/2014/11/23/7-scientifically-proven-benefits-of-gratitude-that-will-motivate-you-to-give-thanks-year-round> (accessed 29/05/2021).

6 Rick Warren, *The Purpose Driven Life: What on earth am I here for?* (Grand Rapids, Zondervan, 2009).

7 J. Richardson, *The Cure for Sorrow: A book of blessings for times of grief* (Orlando: Wanton Gospeller Press, 2016), p. 10.

8 J. O'Donohue, *Benedictus: A book of blessings* (London: Transworld Ireland, 2007), p. 225.

9 J. Pollock, *If Only: Finding contentment in the face of lack and longing* (London: Good Book Company, 2020), p. 141.

10 P. Greig, *Dirty Glory: Go where your best prayers take you* (Colorado Springs: Navpress, 2016), p. 31.

11 F. Buechner, *Secrets in the Dark: A life in sermons* (London: Harper Collins 2006), p. 240.

About Kintsugi Hope.

Kintsugi Hope is a charity founded by Patrick and Diane Regan which longs to bring a message of hope for all those struggling and an assurance that it's OK to acknowledge that you are not OK.

Kintsugi Hope trains churches to run Wellbeing Groups in their communities and online. These groups provide safe and supportive spaces for those who are finding life overwhelming. They are places where people who struggle with mental and emotional health challenges are not only accepted and understood, but are given the tools to grow and flourish in community with others.

The aim of these groups, working through local churches, is to foster an attitude of humility - not to judge, fix or rescue, but to be alongside and love one another. Groups will journey together to look at being honest with each other, how to understand and handle our emotions, building healthy relationships and growing in resilience.

To find out more about the work of Kintsugi Hope and the Wellbeing Groups, visit our website.

The Big Church Read

Did you know that you can read

AND YET

as a Big Church Read?

Join together with friends, your small group or your whole church, or do it on your own, as Rachael Newham leads you through the book.

Visit www.thebigchurchread.co.uk or use the QR code below to watch exclusive videos from Rachael Newham as she explores the ideas and themes of *And Yet.*

The Big Church Read will also provide you with a reading plan and discussion questions to help guide you through the book.

It's free to join in and a great way to read through *And Yet!*

FORM IS A SPIRITUAL
FORMATION IMPRINT
OF SPCK

As well as being an award-winning publisher, SPCK is the oldest Anglican mission agency in the world.

Our mission is to lead the way in creating books and resources that help everyone to make sense of faith.

Will you partner with us to put good books into the hands of prisoners, great assemblies in front of schoolchildren, help create small groups resources for our Home Groups website and reach out to people who have not yet been touched by the Christian faith?

To donate, please visit www.spckpublishing.co.uk/donate or call our friendly fundraising team on 020 7592 3900.

ALSO FROM **RACHAEL NEWHAM**

In this heart-wrenching and inspiring memoir, Rachael Newham tells her story of journeying with depression, anxiety and suicidal thoughts – and how, even in her darkest hours, a flicker of faith lived on.

With unflinching realism and complete honesty, she shows us what it looks like to live with mental illness, and how God can rescue us from even the most desperate of places.

'A truly precious read.'
WILL VAN DER HART

'A beautifully written, hope-filled tale.'
KATHARINE WELBY-ROBERTS

'Rachael's story is testament to God's faithfulness, the love of her family and friends and her own breathtaking courage.'
JO SWINNEY

GET YOUR
COPY